T0361238

ROUTLEDGE LIBRARY EDITIONS:
ENERGY ECONOMICS

Volume 11

THE IMPACT OF JOINT VENTURES ON BIDDING FOR OFFSHORE OIL

THE IMPACT OF JOINT VENTURES ON BIDDING FOR OFFSHORE OIL

JOHN DOUGLASS KLEIN

Routledge
Taylor & Francis Group

LONDON AND NEW YORK

First published in 1983 by Garland Publishing, Inc.

This edition first published in 2018
by Routledge
2 Park Square, Milton Park, Abingdon, Oxon OX14 4RN

and by Routledge
711 Third Avenue, New York, NY 10017

Routledge is an imprint of the Taylor & Francis Group, an informa business

© 1983 John Douglass Klein

British Library Cataloguing in Publication Data
A catalogue record for this book is available from the British Library

ISBN: 978-1-138-10476-1 (Set)
ISBN: 978-1-315-14526-6 (Set) (ebk)
ISBN: 978-1-138-50075-4 (Volume 11) (hbk)
ISBN: 978-1-315-14397-2 (Volume 11) (ebk)

Publisher's Note
The publisher has gone to great lengths to ensure the quality of this reprint but points out that some imperfections in the original copies may be apparent.

Disclaimer
The publisher has made every effort to trace copyright holders and would welcome correspondence from those they have been unable to trace.

The Impact of Joint Ventures on Bidding for Offshore Oil

John Douglass Klein

Garland Publishing, Inc.
New York & London, 1983

Library of Congress Cataloging in Publication Data

Klein, John Douglass.
   The impact of joint ventures on bidding for offshore oil.

   (Outstanding dissertations in economics)
   Bibliography: p.
   1. Offshore oil industry—United States.   2. Oil and gas
leases—United States.   3. Contracts, Letting of—United
States.   4. Joint ventures—United States.   I. Title.
II. Series.
HD9565.K57   1983   333.33'9   79-7939
ISBN 0-8240-4190-9

All volumes in this series are printed on acid-free,
250-year-life paper.

Printed in the United States of America

THE IMPACT OF JOINT VENTURES ON BIDDING

FOR OFFSHORE OIL

BY

JOHN DOUGLASS KLEIN

A thesis submitted in partial fulfillment of the

requirements for the degree of

DOCTOR OF PHILOSOPHY

Economics

at the

UNIVERSITY OF WISCONSIN - MADISON

1975

REVISED GARLAND EDITION

1981

PREFACE TO THE GARLAND EDITION

Since 1975, when this dissertation was first completed, both the theory and practice of outer continental shelf (OCS) leasing have seen significant developments. New bidding methods have been proposed, such as profit sharing; and some have been tested, such as royalty bidding, and bonus bidding with a sliding scale royalty. The OCS Lands Act has been amended. New areas of the OCS have been opened to bidding in the Atlantic and Alaska, and the debate continues over the environmental impact of leasing tracts off California. Interior Secretary James Watt is proposing an increased leasing schedule that even some industry representatives feel is too fast paced.

Amid these issues, the problem of what, if anything, to do about joint ventures remains. At one extreme, joint venture bidding would appear to be the only way that smaller companies, can "get a piece of the action" at an acceptable level of cost and risk. At the other extreme, bidding joint ventures among the nations largest oil companies were judged in 1975 to be enough of a threat to competition that they were banned.

Much of the original work in this dissertation was completed prior to the 1975 ban on joint bidding by majors. The main thrust of the thesis was, and remains, to investigate joint venture participants in OCS sales from institutional, theoretical, and statistical points of view. These views are presented, respectively, in

Chapters II, III and IV. For the Garland edition, all of the statistical work in the dissertation has been revised and brought up to date. Appendix A updates nearly all of the tables and results in Chapter IV, and presents revised figures on the estimated loss in government revenue due to the joint bidding ban. Appendix B contains an entirely new study of the joint bidding ban, which reviews the principal study which led to the ban, and several studies since which are critical of the ban. The major conclusion of Appendix B is that the ban has, in important ways, contributed to the competitiveness of OCS sales.

The bibliography has also been revised and expanded to reflect new contributions not only in the area of joint venture bidding, but theoretical and statistical studies of OCS leasing in general.

One final part of the dissertation which must be revised and expanded is the list of acknowledgements. My advisor, Len Weiss, continues to prod and offer words of encouragement when he can, and I value these words. Ken Erickson, of the Office of Leasing Policy at the U. S. Department of Energy was invaluable in providing me with many up-to-the-minute references regarding OCS leasing policies. Ken also introduced me to John Lohrenz of the U. S. Geological Survey, who is a fount of information on OCS sales. John Lohrenz helped me acquire the U.S. Geological Survey's LPR (Lease, Production and Revenue) data tapes, without which this revision would have been impossible. He also was kind enough to invite me

to a "Data Analysis Workshop for Mineral Leases," held August 17, 1979
in Washington, D.C., and co-sponsored by the Los Alamos Scientific
Laboratory, and the U.S. Geological Survey. Brian Ellsworth, one
of my students at Union College, was a great help in updating some
of the statistical work in Chapter IV. I also extend my thanks
to Peter Etherden for his helpful and thoughtful comments on an
earlier version of the work in Appendix B.

I have to thank Ted Schwartz, Scott Levine and Julie Swant of
the Union College Computing Center for their patient replies to my
all-too-frequent questions. The many revisions to the thesis were
typed by Laura Meirowitz and Nancy Angus.

Last, but far from least, I must thank my wife, Adrienne. She
was not only an understanding and supportive friend, but also an
invaluable assistant, as proofreader and editor.

In spite of my efforts, some errors must surely remain, and I
continue to take sole responsibility for them.

                                    Schenectady, NY
                                    August, 1981

TABLE OF CONTENTS

The problems posed by joint venture bidding for offshore oil were first brought to my attention by Professor Leonard W. Weiss during his Industrial Organization seminar in the Fall of 1970. In the Summer of 1972 I chose this area to be the topic of my dissertation research.

The study of offshore leasing sales goes far beyond the field of economics, including such areas as geology and geophysics, finance, law, politics, statistics and psychology. This study focuses on the economic aspects of bidding for offshore oil, with special emphasis on the nature and role of joint ventures. Certain of the results, particularly the theoretical model of bidding with asymmetric information in Chapter III, would apply to any sealed bidding situation in which the exact value of the object offered for sale was unknown. The results here are all phrased in terms of a high-bid-wins situation, but could be adapted with minor changes to sealed bid sales where the low bidder wins.

In the time I have spent working on this project, I have incurred many debts. My first thanks must go to my major professor, Leonard W. Weiss, for his advice, and his patience. My other committee members, Charles Cicchetti and Kenneth R. Smith, have also provided valuable comments and encouragement. Theodore Groves served on my committee until 1973, and was particularly helpful in working out the theoretical model. Arthur S. Goldberger pointed out to me the relationship between sealed bid auctions and order statistics.

A great debt of gratitude must go to representatives of six oil companies, who asked to remain anonymous. Interviews conducted in November and December of 1973 provided insights into the workings of the offshore oil industry without which this dissertation would have been impossible. Interviews with John Rankin, Director of the Outer Continental Shelf Office of the Bureau of Land Management, and J. Rogers Pearcy of the U. S. Geological Survey were also highly informative.

On the technical side, my thanks go to Keith Brown of Purdue University, who provided the data for some of the early sales on punched cards. Jean Torgeson was tireless in helping to finish the keypunching. Marianne Miller typed an early draft, and Mary Jo Fairbanks did a beautiful job typing the final draft, in spite of an intolerable number of tables. To my parents go thanks for help in proofreading, and for all their support.

As must always be the case, I take full responsibility for all errors which remain.

LIST OF TABLES

LIST OF FIGURES

CHAPTER I

INTRODUCTION

1. Purpose of the Study

This study examines the effect on competition of permitting
joint ventures to bid in federal offshore oil and gas leasing sales.
Western economists and policy makers generally contend that
competition is desirable, since it promotes, in the absence of
outside controls, efficient allocation and use of resources.
Difficulties arise, however, in judging which policies advocated
by public servants tend to promote competition, and which to
restrain it; or more accurately, judging which policies promote
desirable ends, and which do not. Weighing the desirability of
joint ventures in bidding for offshore oil poses just such a problem.

The two sides of the issue are easily stated. Advocates of
joint venture bidding stress the enormous costs and risks involved
in exploring for offshore oil. They argue that small firms can
participate in offshore sales only by allowing them to form joint
ventures, and that large firms are made more potent competitors
when they combine. Hollis M. Dole, Assistant Secretary of the
Interior, expressed this position in his response to a question
concerning the impact of allowing joint ventures to bid on
competition, posed by Senator Philip Hart:

Joint bidding, whether by major or independent oil
companies, is permitted because joint ventures are
an established approach to mineral exploration. This
is true not only in the OCS, but onshore as well.
The present system recognizes the substantial risks
and high costs attendant to offshore mineral exploration and, by spreading these risks and costs over as
large a number of wildcat exposures as possible, it
(1) permits entry of smaller firms who could not
compete otherwise,
(2) permits larger firms to be competitive over a
greater number of tracts,
(3) increases the bonuses received by the Federal
Government, and
(4) lessens the amount of money risked on each tract
by each company.
Joint bidding increases competition by enabling more
small companies to bid.[1]

On the other side of the issue, many firms which now enter partner-

ships could and would participate in sales even without forming joint

ventures. In addition, joint ventures for bidding might provide

settings for exchanging too much information. Firms might reach

tacit or overt agreements concerning later production or marketing

which could be termed anti-competitive. A. D. Neale, in his intro-

duction to The Antitrust Laws of the United States, sums up the

skeptical view:

Competition between firms is, after all, accounted
a principal virtue of private economic activity,
operating as a stimulus to improved methods and as a
safeguard against indifference to the wishes of the
consumers. ...Even if it is accepted that there may be
situations in which, for example, rationalization of
production in larger units should be promoted and
competition may justifiably be lessened or restrained,
it seems questionable whether the job of deciding
which these situations are and what form of restraint
to adopt should be left to those upon whom competition
is expected to exercise a salutary influence.[2]

The arguments for and against joint venture bidding tend to

rely upon the effect of joint ventures on the number of bidders

in a sale. But more bidders in a sale does not necessarily
mean more competition and higher winning bids, nor do fewer bidders
imply less competition, since some bidders may be more vigorous
competitors than others. That is, some bidders can and do place
competitive bids on a greater number of tracts than other bidders.
In this study of offshore leasing, both the number and the relative
competitiveness of bidders will be examined in order to judge the
degree of competition in the sales, and in order to pass some
judgement on the Department of Interior policy toward joint ventures
as it affects competition.

The Department's joint venture policy was, for many years, set
forth in the original law which set up the federal leasing program
in 1953. The law states that no bidder may violate the U. S. Code,
Title 18, section 1860 regarding bids at land sales:

> Whoever bargains, contracts or agrees, or attempts to
> bargain, contract or agree with another that such other
> shall not bid upon or purchase any parcel of land of
> the United States offered at public sale; or Whoever, by
> intimidation, combination, or unfair management, hinders,
> prevents, or attempts to hinder or prevent, any person
> from bidding upon or purchasing any tract of land so
> offered for sale;
> Shall be fined not more than $1,000 or imprisoned
> not more than one year, or both.[3]

This law has never been invoked to prevent companies from combining
for the purpose of bidding in offshore leasing sales.

Following the California offshore sale in February 1968, the
Antitrust Division of the Department of Justice speculated that
something should be done about joint ventures.[4] In that sale,
the majority of tracts were won by one of two bidders: the first,

a combination of Humble (now Exxon), Arco, and Chevron; and the other a joint venture of Union, Gulf, Texaco and Mobil. The Antitrust Division advanced the hypothesis that if those firms had not been permitted to form joint ventures, they would have bid independently, and bidding would have been more competitive, evidenced by higher winning bids. The Division was not able, however, to provide any evidence in support of the conjecture.

In recent sales, joint venture bidding has become more and more prevalent. The proportion of bids placed by joint ventures has risen from 18 percent in the first sale in 1954 to 82 percent in the sale held in June, 1973. With this dramatic increase in mind, the Department of Interior has been taking a new look at the impact of joint ventures. In a recent interview with the New York Times, Darius Gaskins, the department's coordinator of outer continental shelf programs, argued in favor of a proposed ban on joint ventures among major oil companies. His argument was that the ban would increase the number of bidders, and "we do better when there are more competitors... When there are six bidders, we do much better than when there are two bidders, regardless of who the bidders are."[5]

Plans for such a ban on major joint ventures have been in the works for some time now. In April, 1974, the Interior Department announced that all companies controlling worldwide reserves in excess of 5 billion barrels would be prohibited from forming partnerships with one another.[6] This regulation would have banned joint ventures among the seven largest oil companies, although any of these companies would still be permitted to join with smaller firms. The seven companies which would have been covered by the proposed ban were Exxon, Shell, Mobil, Gulf, Texaco, Chevron and Amoco. That order was never put into effect, however, and in January, 1975, the Department of Interior announced a revised ban, which will cover all firms having worldwide hydrocarbon production equivalent to 1.5 million barrels per day of crude petroleum or more.[7] The revised order is scheduled to take effect prior to the July, 1975 Gulf of Mexico offshore sale, and will cover the same seven firms included under the original proposal, with the addition of an eighth, Atlantic Richfield.

With all of the current interest in offshore oil, and the problems of joint venture bidding, this thesis will examine the bidding behavior of joint ventures, and will attempt to determine whether or not joint ventures, and in particular joint ventures involving large firms, are beneficial or harmful to competition.

2. Plan of the Study

This study examines the problem of joint venture bidding in both institutional and theoretical frameworks. Chapter II takes a lengthy look at the institution of offshore leasing sales, and the role of joint ventures therein. The remaining chapters are devoted to the development and testing of a theory of joint venture bidding. Finally, conclusions and suggestions for additional work are set forth.

Chapter II contains three sections. First, the role of government in offshore leasing is presented. This section includes a summary of the laws governing the leasing of federal land and a discussion of the current role of the Interior Department conducting offshore sales. The next section describes techniques used by the oil industry in exploring and developing offshore tracts, including use of geological and geophysical exploration techniques, as they apply to evaluating a tract, bid preparation, bidding strategies, and the development and operation of leased tracts. The third part of Chapter II investigates the reasons for, and methods of joint venture formation, including some of the common provisions of a joint venture agreement.

Chapter III begins with a review of the literature on competitive bidding. Some of this literature deals with the problem of bidding in general, while some is addressed specifically to the problem of bidding in offshore leasing sales. The main theoretical results are also presented in Chapter III. The object of the proposed theory is to include institutional aspects of joint ventures which affect their bidding behavior, in a general theory of bidding.

A model is developed, first in the absence of joint ventures, and then with joint ventures included. The model is basically a Cournot-type model in which the behavior of each bidder depends on the behavior of all other bidders, and a Nash equilibrium is shown to exist. The primary theoretical feature of a joint venture involving at least one major oil company is the additional information available to a bidding unit when several firms, each of which has gathered information independently, join forces. The increase in information reduces the risk faced by the joint venture, and enables it to bid more confidently. The bidding model is used to simulate an offshore sale, and three testable hypotheses are stated:

(1) Joint ventures with superior information win with a greater share of their bids than other bidders,

(2) Average winning bids are the same for all bidders,

(3) Average non-winning bids are greater for better informed joint ventures than for other bidders.

Chapter IV tests the proposed hypotheses after a description of the available data. The statistical results reported include a tabulation of the success of various types of bidders, including joint ventures, in offshore sales. Also, regression analysis is used to explain the variance in both winning and non-winning bids. The last two sections of Chapter IV use the regression results to estimate the impact of several policies to limit the formation of joint ventures, on government revenue.

Chapter V concludes the study. Joint ventures which include major oil companies do bid more successfully than other bidders, and they also place higher bids in losing than others. These joint ventures tend, however, to pay more than other bidders for tracts of comparable quality. Although the costs of banning certain types of joint ventures is found to be relatively small, the benefits may

also be small. In particular, the Department of Interior assertion
that increased numbers of bidders leads to higher government
revenues is questioned. The thesis ends with a few suggestions
for further research.

FOOTNOTES

1. U. S. Congress, Senate, Committee on the Judiciary, Sub-committee on Antitrust and Monopoly, Governmental Intervention in the Market Mechanism, The Petroleum Industry, Part 5: Federally Owned Oil and Gas Lands on the Outer Continental Shelf. (91st Congress, 2nd session, August 11 and 13, 1970, pursuant to Senate Resolution 40) (Washington: Government Printing Office, 1970), p. 2254.

2. A. D. Neale, The Antitrust Laws of the United States. (2nd ed; Cambridge: Cambridge University Press, 1970), pp. 1, 2.

3. 18 U.S.C. 1970 ed.   1860.

4. The problem of joint venture bidding was first brought to my attention by Professor Leonard W. Weiss, University of Wisconsin, who spent the academic year 1969-70 with the Antitrust Division of the Department of Justice.

5. Quoted in Edward Cowan, "U. S. Plans to Prohibit Joint Bidding for Offshore Leases by 8 Big Companies," The New York Times, January 5, 1975, p. 31.

6. U. S. Department of Interior, "Outer Continental Shelf Lands Act: Proposal on Oil and Gas Leases," Federal Register, Vol. 39, No. 80 (April 24, 1974), pp. 14511-14512.

7. U. S. Department of Interior, "Qualified Joint Bidders," Federal Register, Vol. 30, No. 6 (Feb. 21, 1975), pp. 7673-7676.

CHAPTER II

THE INSTITUTIONS OF OFFSHORE LEASING SALES

An analysis of joint bidding in offshore sales is of more than
passing interest. From 1953, when the federal government initiated
its offshore leasing program, through 1973, over 30 oil and gas
sales were held, offering 20 million acres, over half of which have
been bid on and leased; and bonuses have totaled over 13 billion
dollars. Table 2-1 indicates the growing size and frequency of
offshore sales. As has already been noted, the participation of
bidding partnerships or joint ventures in these sales has been on
the rise throughout the history of the sales.

In 1970, about 17 percent of domestic crude petroleum production came from offshore, up from only two percent in 1954.[1] The
continental shelf represents the last frontier for new sources of
domestic oil and gas in the lower 48 states, and the concern expressed in recent years regarding energy self-sufficiency for the U. S.
is reflected in the greatly stepped up leasing program now planned by
the Department of Interior. Former Interior Secretary R. C. B. Morton
has indicated that the Department plans to move from the one million
acres offered in 1973 to a rate of perhaps five million acres by
1975, and ten million acres for the following few years.[2]

The literature on competitive bidding, and on offshore leasing
provides little insight into the role of joint ventures in federal
offshore sales. This chapter presents information gathered from

TABLE 2-1. STATISTICAL SUMMARY OF OFFSHORE SALES[a]

(1) Sale Date	(2) Pct. Wildcat[b]	(3) Location	(4) Acres Leased[c] (tho)[c]	(5) Tracts Leased[c]	(6) Total Bonus Paid ($ mil)	(7) Ave. Bonus ($ tho) (6)/(5)	(8) No. of Tracts Bid On[d]	(9) Total # of Bids[e]	(10) Total All Bids ($ mil)	(11) Ave. Bid ($ tho) (10)/(9)	(12) Ave. No. Bids per Tract (9)/(8)
10/13/54	100.	LA	394	90	116.	1293.	90	327	288.	882.	3.6
11/ 9/54	100.	TX	67	19	23.	1229.	19	90	74.	820.	4.7
7/12/55	100.	LA,TX	402	121	109.	897.	121	384	323.	842.	3.2
5/26/59	100.	FL	132	23	2.	74.	23	23	2.	74.	1.0
8/11/59	0.	LA	38	19	88.	4633.	19	45	172.	3820.	2.4
2/24/60	100.	LA,TX	704	147	283.	1923.	173	444	575.	1295.	2.6
3/13/62	100.	LA	951	206	177.	860.	211	538	314.	584.	2.5
3/16/62	100.	LA,TX	954	205	268.	1309.	210	666	605.	909.	3.2
10/ 9/62	0.	LA	16	9	44.	4876.	14	26	66.	2549.	1.9
5/14/63	100.	CA	312	57	13.	225.	58	70	14.	200.	1.2
4/28/64	0.	LA	32	23	60.	2624.	23	69	94.	1360.	3.0
10/ 1/64	100.	OR,WA	580	101	36.	352.	101	223	54.	240.	2.2
3/29/66	0.	LA	35	17	89.	5226.	18	64	275.	4303.	3.6
10/18/66	0.	LA	104	24	99.	4132.	32	79	185.	2344.	2.5
12/15/66	0.	CA	1	1	21.	21189.	1	7	90.	12848.	7.0
6/13/67	100.	LA	744	158	510.	3228.	172	742	1628.	2194.	4.3
2/ 6/68	100.	CA	363	71	603.	8489.	75	164	1294.	7888.	2.2
5/21/68	100.	TX	541	110	596.	5417.	141	556	1620.	2914.	3.9
11/19/68	0.	LA	29	16	150.	9367.	21	38	398.	10485.	1.8
1/14/69	0.	LA	48	20	44.	2202.	26	40	71.	1776.	1.5
12/16/69	0.	LA	60	16	67.	4182.	16	58	230.	3973.	3.6
7/21/70	0.	LA	44	19	98.	5146.	21	59	163.	2770.	2.8
12/15/70	100.	LA	553	119	847.	7120.	127	1043	2877.	2759.	8.2
11/ 4/71	0.	LA	37	11	96.	8755.	13	33	173.	5234.	2.5
9/12/72	100.	LA	290	62	586.	9449.	74	324	1599.	4936.	4.4
12/19/72	100.	LA	535	116	1666.	14358.	119	690	6191.	8973.	5.8
6/19/73	95.	LA,TX	547	100	1591.	15914.	104	551	6248.	11340.	5.3

(1)	(2)	(3)	(4)	(5)	(6)	(7)	(8)	(9)	(10)	(11)	(12)
12/20/73	87.	AL,FL	485	87	1491.	17139.	89	373	3405.	9128.	4.2
3/28/74	82.	AL,LA	421	91	2093.	22995.	114	402	6474.	16104.	3.5
5/29/74	99.	LA,TX	565	102	1472.	14428.	123	352	3354.	9529.	2.9
7/30/74	90.	AL,LA,TX	100	19	30.	1591.	49	57	89.	1558.	1.2
10/16/74	93.	AL,LA	634	136	1427.	10494.	149	330	2515.	7620.	2.2
2/ 4/75	97.	TX	626	113	275.	2431.	143	281	485.	1725.	2.0
5/28/75	82.	AL,LA,TX	406	86	233.	2708.	102	191	403.	2109.	1.9
7/29/75	80.	LA,TX	336	66	163.	2473.	80	179	317.	1771.	2.2
12/11/75	100.	CA	310	56	417.	7452.	70	166	902.	5433.	2.4
2/18/76	49.	FL,LA,TX	161	34	176.	5176.	41	81	428.	5284.	2.0
4/13/76	100.	AK	409	76	560.	7366.	81	244	1732.	7099.	3.0
8/17/76	100.	DE,NJ	529	93	1128.	12128.	101	410	3513.	8569.	4.1
11/16/76	0.	AL,LA,TX	178	43	379.	8818.	48	117	833.	7120.	2.4
6/23/77	62.	LA,TX	605	124	1170.	9436.	152	424	2928.	6906.	2.8
10/27/77	100.	AK	324	57	388.	6816.	61	142	644.	4532.	2.3
3/28/78	100.	FL,GA	244	43	101.	2343.	57	99	151.	1525.	1.7
4/25/78	45.	LA,TX	438	90	734.	8152.	101	283	1559.	5510.	2.8
10/31/78	100.	FL	201	35	61.	1748.	35	62	88.	1413.	1.8
12/19/78	75.	LA,TX	412	81	871.	10759.	88	288	2355.	8178.	3.3
2/28/79	100.	DE,MD,NJ	222	39	40.	1026.	44	73	66.	901.	1.7
6/29/79	98.	CA	288	54	573.	10608.	55	112	995.	8881.	2.0
7/31/79	64.	LA,TX	391	81	1247.	15401.	88	316	3334.	10551.	3.6
All Sales	86.		16820	3486	23311.	6687.	3893	12335	62194.	5042.	3.2

aSource: U. S. Department of Interior, Geological Survey, LPR-5 data tape.

bPercentage of tracts leased designated "wildcat," as opposed to "drainage" or "development".

cIncludes all tracts receiving bonus bids. (Excludes 8 tracts in the 10/16/75, and 30 tracts in the 10/27/77 sale which were leased by royalty bidding.)

dIncludes bonus-bid tracts leased by the government. (Excludes same tracts as in note c.)

eIncludes all bonus bids received by the government. (Excludes 57 royalty bids in the 10/16/75 sale and 98 royalty bids in the 10/27/77 sale.)

industry and government publications, and from a series of interviews with industry and government spokesmen on the formation and behavior of joint ventures.[3]

1. The Role of Government in Offshore Leasing[4]

The first systematic offshore leasing program in the United States was adopted by the state of Louisiana in August, 1945. This "Modern Leasing Program" as it was called, was designed to promote orderly development of the Louisiana offshore mineral resources. Later in the same year, President Truman ordered by proclamation that the natural resources of the sea bed of the continental shelf were to be controlled by the United States.

Immediately, a debate arose as to how rights to offshore lands should be divided between the states and the federal government. In United States vs. California (332 U.S. 1947), the Supreme Court set the dividing line at three miles, with the federal government commanding all offshore territory on the continental shelf outside that limit. The question was not to be so simply resolved, however. The state of Louisiana continued to claim a three league (about 10 mile) limit, and also disputed the federal government's definition of the shore line, which at some places on the Gulf of Mexico is indeed a matter of debate. The matter of jurisdiction is to this day not completely settled, although disputed territory has been controlled by the federal government, with revenues being held in escrow.

Federal leasing of offshore lands officially began in 1953 with the passage of, first, the Submerged Lands Act, and then the Outer Continental Shelf Lands Act. The former expressly assigned offshore mineral rights near shore to state control. The law stipulated three miles as the states' boundary on Atlantic and Pacific coasts, and three leagues in the Gulf of Mexico, although as earlier noted, these distances, particularly in the Gulf, are still disputed. The OCS Lands Act extended to the oceans the authority granted to the federal government by the Mineral Leasing Act of 1920. The 1953 act provides that the Bureau of Land Management, a branch of the Department of Interior, hold periodic sealed bid auctions for mineral rights to tracts on the offshore United States.

By law, auctions must be conducted in one of two ways, but until 1974 only one of the two had ever been used. The bidding method generally used by the government has been the so-called bonus bid system. Under this system, sealed bids submitted to the government represent a lump sum payment to the government by the successful bidder, paid at the time of the sale. Associated with the bonus is a fixed percentage royalty on the value of production, paid only in the event that the leased tract proves to be productive. Customarily, the royalty rate has been set at one-sixth (16.67 percent).

The alternative bidding method uses the percentage royalty as the bidding objective. The bidder offering to pay the highest percentage royalty wins the lease, and is also required to pay a small fixed bonus at the time of the sale. Although this bidding method was first used in a federal sale in November 1974, it has been used in state sales by Louisiana and California. For a time, the state of Louisiana even used a system in which both the bonus and the royalty were bidding variables. Determining winners under this system proved hopelessly difficult.

The royalty bidding system has been carefully considered recently, since it requires a much smaller advance payment on the part of bidders, and allows companies to bid on more prospects, knowing that they will have to pay the government substantial sums of money only in the event that the tracts won prove to be productive. The payment of large bonuses for worthless tracts under the bonus bid system is no small expense. In December 1973, a joint venture including Exxon, Mobil and Champlin Petroleum Company paid over $211 million for a tract off the coast of Florida which to date has shown no commercial production.[5]

On the eight tracts leased in November 1974, under the royalty bidding system, high bids ranged from 51.5 percent to 82.1 percent of the value of production from the tracts. One suspects that these tracts would become unprofitable much sooner than tracts on which a lower royalty rate was being paid, since as operating costs begin to rise, profit margins would quickly erode. In particular, it would be surprising to find secondary or tertiary recovery profitable on tracts with such high royalty rates.

The royalty bidding method has not been used extensively in federal sales out of two fears. The first, as just mentioned, concerns the possibility that much oil and gas might be shut in because a high royalty commitment has made its production unprofitable. Second, because a royalty system has much lower initial costs to winning bidders, with no huge bonus payments, the system would permit many smaller, less qualified firms to enter the offshore industry. The bonus represents a barrier which only large, and presumably technically qualified bidders, can overcome. If some way could be devised to identify qualified bidders, independent of their ability to pay a large initial bonus, this second objection to royalty bidding would be eliminated.

One final type of payment, rent, is required regardless of the bidding method employed. Rental is due to the government on all leased land, whether productive or not, and is usually some very minimal fee between three and ten dollars per acre per year. Tracts vary in size, but are generally about 5,000 acres, although they may be halved or quartered for a sale.

The leases run for a period of five years, or so long as a tract is productive, subject to cancellation by the government on thirty days notice for a non-producing tract, and immediately on a producing tract. The threat of cancellation is used primarily to insure that tracts are developed in a responsible manner.

From the first federal sale in 1954 through the 1960's, the tracts to be offered in a sale were determined by the industry.

The government put out a request for nominations of tracts and all interested parties were welcome to make suggestions. The government than tabulated the nominations, and offered for sale those tracts which had been nominated most frequently.

Beginning in March 1970, the government has purchased seismic data covering general areas to be put up for auction.[6] Using this data, the government is able to choose tracts with high oil and gas potential, and is able to offer attractive tracts without relying solely on the nominations from industry members.[7] This refined method of tract selection was made necessary by the industry policy of nominating increasing numbers of acres for each sale in order to disguise their own preferences, as well as to make more offshore land available, making it difficult for the government to select a reasonable number of acres without additional information. The data acquired by the government has also proved useful in evaluating the potential risk to the environment of developing proposed sale areas, a concern which has blossomed since the oil spills in the Santa Barbara channel in 1969, and the 1971 offshore Louisiana drilling platform fire.

When tract selection is completed, the list of tracts to be offered is released to the industry. The typical lag between the call by the government for nominations and the announcement of selected tracts is four to five months. The period of time between tract announcement and the sale date is seven to twelve months, although recently, detailed environmental studies have lengthened this period.[8] During this time, the government holds a public hearing on the environmental impact of the sale and releases an environmental impact statement. At the conclusion of the environmental considerations, a final decision on the sale is made. At this time, some or all of the proposed tracts may be withdrawn due to environmental considerations. Potential bidders use this period to evaluate the specific tracts in the sale and prepare their bids.

In 1968, the Bureau of the Budget reaffirmed a provision in the 1953 OCS Act: that the government should receive fair market value for offshore leases. The Bureau of the Budget, to this end, recommended that the Department of Interior should estimate the value of tracts put up for sale.[9] Interior has in fact made estimates of value for each tract in recent sales using seismic data purchased from commercial companies. These estimates have been used as a guideline for rejection of bids which are deemed too low. Prior to this policy, the government did not attempt to evaluate tracts, and rejected bids only if they fell below some arbitrary (quite low) minimum level.[10]

In another effort to better evaluate offshore tracts, the government will soon require bidders to turn over exploration data which they obtain for their own evaluations.[11] The data which the government now uses is purchased on the market, or generated internally, and government value estimates are frequently at odds with industry estimates. Referring to the December, 1970 sale, Offshore magazine reports that "in case after case, Interior's top

dollar assessment of a tract's value was low in relation to what
was actually paid in bonus money for the tract."[12] At the other
end of the scale, the government has taken a more aggressive posture
on rejecting bids which are not judged to give the "fair market
value" sought. For example, in the March 1974 sale, 23 of 114 high
bids were rejected, of which six were over $5 million, and one was
a bid of $15.8 million.[13]

The complicated process of tract evaluation will be dealt with
in the following section, but it is already clear that a wide
difference of opinion on tract value can arise. The government
hopes that by gathering more data from industry, and on its own,
it can better estimate each tract's value and can thereby be sure
of receiving a fair price for the nation's resources.

2. Methods of Offshore Exploration and Development

Exploration Methods

Before considering the complexities of tract evaluation, it
is instructive to touch on some of the technical aspects of offshore exploration. Most offshore oil and gas exploration in the
U. S. has been in the Gulf of Mexico, off the coast of Louisiana
and Texas. The Gulf represents an extension of the rich oil-
producing geological province found onshore in Louisiana and Texas,
and oil producers naturally looked to the Gulf in the 1940's as a
potential oil area. Not surprisingly, the Gulf has proved a highly
productive area for oil and gas. Offshore exploration has also

occurred off the coasts of Washington, Oregon, California, Mississippi, Alabama, Florida (Gulf side), and Alaska, and the industry is anxious to begin exploring off the Atlantic coast, as soon as environmental and federal versus state ownership difficulties are cleared up. The Gulf of Mexico, however, has been by far the major offshore petroleum province in the United States.

The federal government readily grants exploration permits for offshore lands. These permits allow the grantee to do any exploration which does not involve puncturing the sea floor. Thus any evaluation of the hydrocarbon content of a tract must be done by inference, since the government does not permit drilling prior to a sale, to see whether oil or gas is actually present. Offshore explorers have several tools available, falling into two categories: geological and geophysical. Geology refers to the history of the earth as recorded in its rocks. By examining rocks, and the layers of rocks present at a point, geologists can infer the history of the area, and whether hydrocarbons are likely to be found nearby. Geophysics deals with the physics of the earth. Geophysical exploration techniques include magnetic, galvanometric (or gravimetric), electric and seismic surveys. These techniques can be conducted from the surface, and permit inferences to be drawn about the subsurface geology.

Since offshore exploration is only permitted from the surface geophysical techniques, notable seismic survey, are most frequently employed. Seismic proves to be a particularly effective method offshore for two reasons. First, it is physically very easy to use. A ship can easily tow a seismic mapping device back and forth in a grid fashion over the area to be explored. Second, most hydrocarbon deposits offshore occur in salt domes. A salt dome causes an upward bulging of subsurface rocks, known as an anticline, which often traps hydrocarbons (see Figure 2-1). These structures show up very clearly in seismic mapping. Not only is this type of structure fairly easy to spot, but recent advances in seismic technology actually permit geophysicists to predict with improving accuracy the presence of hydrocarbons. This so-called "bright spot" technology is the rage of the offshore industry. Its discovery is claimed by several oil companies, and its use is rapidly becoming universal. Although not 100 percent reliable, it is a vast improvement over previous techniques for estimating whether or not hydrocarbons are present.[14]

One of the most important tools to the offshore explorer is subsurface geological information. As indicated, subsurface geological exploration, such as core sampling, is not permitted on unleased tracts. Leased tracts, however, may be explored thoroughly, and geological features may be extrapolated from known areas into unknown areas. For this reason, bidders who already have leased tracts in an area are at an advantage in trying to evaluate additional tracts put up for sale in that area. In fact, information gleaned from drilling leased tracts is closely guarded, since such information improves the position of the firm for future

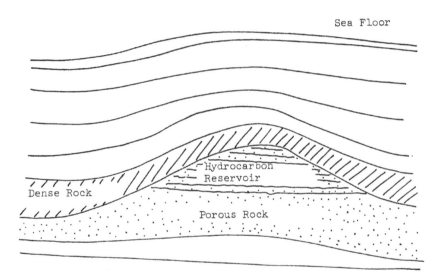

Figure 2-1. Cross Section of an Anticline, such as
Formed by a Salt Dome.

sales. Possessing information from adjacent tracts (called off-setting tracts), often makes a firm very desirable as a partner in a joint venture in the subsequent sale of those tracts.

Bidding in an offshore sale is a process of continually refining information, until bids can at last be constructed. When the government releases the list of tracts to be offered for sale, bidders must decide which tracts warrant detailed study, and which are not likely prospects for oil and gas. These preliminary decisions are usually made with the aid of an initial seismic survey of the entire leasing area. To save initial expense, firms potentially interested in bidding in a sale often perform this survey jointly, in what is called a "group shoot." The word "shoot" refers to the old method of gathering seismic data, in which a series of explosions was set off.

While this survey provides little detail, it generally locates any potential oil-bearing structure of reasonable size. Where such structures appear, bidders independently obtain additional detailed seismic data, and draw subsurface maps, showing the size and shape of each structure. The firms also study any peculiarities of the structure, such as faulting, and identify the likely locations for hydrocarbons. After collecting all of the data, the first step in placing a dollar value on a tract begins: an estimation of the hydrocarbon reserves in the structure.

Tract Evaluation

Table 2-2 contains the bids on four typical tracts from four leasing sales. The wide range of bids on each tract is not particularly unusual - bids for a single tract frequently differ by a multiple of several hundred. Two questions naturally arise: how do bidders evaluate offshore tracts; and what leads bidders to make such different bids for the same tract of land?

There are as many methods for evaluating offshore tracts as there are offshore explorers. The object in all cases is the same: to provide the bidding unit a profitable investment. A bidder could easily make high bids which would win every tract in a sale, but it would be unlikely that such bids would result in a profitable investment. On the other side of the coin, anyone who bids low, expecting to make large profits, would face the prospect of winning few if any tracts.

Tract evaluation is crucial to each bidder. The evaluation tells the firms how much they can afford to bid and still receive an acceptable return on their investment. This section focuses on tract evaluation and how the differences in value estimates, which the bids in Table 2-2 reflect, can arise.

An estimate of reserves involves not only guessing how much oil is in the ground, but how much of it can be recovered, at what cost, and at what rate. These factors also depend on the characteristics of the structure, and can be estimated by comparisons with similar, previously leased and drilled structures.

TABLE 2-2. SUMMARY OF BIDS ON FOUR SELECTED TRACTS*

1		2	
$2,003,000.00	Gulf	$11,460,844.00	Tenneco
1,750,155.00	(Pure, Ohio, Sun)	9,740,000.00	(Brit. Am., Richfield, Miss. River Fuel, Union)
382,000.00	Humble		
215,000.00	Shell	7,111,200.00	(Gulf, Mobil)
166,650.00	St. Indiana	2,501,387.82	Sinclair
85,250.00	St. California	813,750.00	Shell
		593,000.00	(Signal, Louisiana Land Expl., Allied Chem., Amerada)
		542,500.00	Union Prod.
		502,354.00	(Kerr, McGee, Felmont, Sunray, Delhi-Taylor, Jos. E. Seagram)
		244,680.00	(Atlantic, Cities Service)
		169,452.00	Pan American

(continued on next page)

*The selected tracts are: 1, #0413, leased 10/13/54;
2, #1134, leased 3/16/62;
3, #2479, leased 12/20/73;
4, #2658, leased 5/29/74.

Source: Statistical Summary of Offshore Sales.

TABLE 2-2. (continued)

3		4	
$126,778,350.00	(Mobil, Champlain, Exxon)	$70,664,000.00	(Chevron, Tenneco, Samedan)
61,166,000.00	(Texaco, Tenneco, Gulf, Columbia Gas)	8,760,000.00	(Felmont, Kerr McGee, General American, Cabot, Highland Resources, Transocean Oil, Case Pomeroy, LVO, Unidel, Weeks Nat. Res.)
51,374,534.40	Sun		
25,438,000.00	(Continental, Phillips, Shell Drillamex, Florida Gas Barber)		
17,799,955.20	Occidental	7,238,000.00	(Shell, Texas Gulf, Northern Nat. Gas)
15,146,000.00	(Union, Chevron, Amoco)	5,568,480.00	(Superior, Canadian Superior)
12,844,800.00	(Cities Service, Skelly, Pennzoil Oil and Gas, Mesa, Pennzoil L and T)	3,726,000.00	(Continental, Arco)
		1,707,000.00	Allied Chemical
6,180,000.00	(Amarada Hess, Louisiana Land Expl., Marathon, Texas East., La. Land Offshore)		
5,137,920.00	(Allied Chem., Clark, Sonat, Tesoro)		
504,057.60	Murphy Oil Co.		

After the structure is mapped, with all of the faults drawn in, then the real guesswork begins. What is the area of the pay zone (hydrocarbon producing zone), and how thick is it? This may be difficult to estimate, since some structures have a series of paying sands. There may be only one, or there may be as many as 25 levels of hydrocarbon bearing sands stacked one on top of another, while only the top one shows up in a seismic survey. The **porosity** of the sand must also be estimated, to determine how much <u>room</u> there is for the oil. What is the saturation of the pay zone with water and other impurities? What is the pressure? What kinds of hydrocarbons are present: oil, gas or both? What percentage of the hydrocarbons are recoverable? All of these questions must be answered by looking at maps and well logs of similar structures already drilled, and all are conditioned on the overriding assumption, that the structure does indeed contain hydrocarbons.

Perhaps most important, geologists must estimate the probability of finding any hydrocarbons at all in a structure. A structure may seem of ideal shape and size, but surface techniques can never say for certain whether hydrocarbons are actually present. The question of estimating reserves is done presuming that hydrocarbons are present. To complete the evaluation, this figure must be multiplied times the probability of finding oil at all. To analyze the probability of finding oil in a given structure, geologists refer to information about past success with structures of that type. From this past information, geologists report that

of all similar structures drilled in the past, some proportion have
yielded hydrocarbons, and this proportion is an indication of the
probability of finding hydrocarbons in the present structure.

To sum up, reserve estimates are based on a number of different parameters:[15]

Estimated reserves = (Probability of hydrocarbons)

$\times$ (area of reservoir)

$\times$ (average thickness of pay zone)

$\times$ (number of pay zones)

$\times$ (porosity)

$\times$ (1 - water saturation)

$\times$ (recovery factor).

Offshore structures are well enough defined that about 1/3 of all
federal leases granted are productive. Not all are necessarily
profitable, but at least producing oil from them recoups losses.
This is a rather remarkable figure in light of the 1 in 10 success
figure commonly quoted for onshore operations'.

This high success ratio is due first to the combination of
very clearly defined structures plus ideal mapping conditions
(water is a perfect medium on which to gather seismic data), which
result in excellent seismic maps of the subsurface. Secondly,
the high expense of leasing, exploring, and producing offshore
justifies a much more careful study of the prospects than would
be warranted onshore. Finally, the new bright spot analysis has
been employed, in varying degrees of success, by most bidders.

The presence of a bright spot is a necessary, but not sufficient indication of the presence of hydrocarbons. Unfortunately, substances other than hydrocarbons can produce bright spots.

To place a cash value on the estimate of reserves, forecasts of prices, costs, and production rates must be made. Also a discount rate must be chosen. The discounted present value (DPV) of a tract is calculated as follows, where production and cost is assumed to occur at some point in time t in the future:

$$DPV = (\text{Estimated Reserves}) \times (\text{Net Price}) \times e^{-rt}$$

where Net Price = (Unit Price - Unit Cost) and "r" is the Discount Rate.[16]

Bid Preparation

In a world of perfect certainty and competition, the equilibrium price of a tract would equal the discounted present value, with r set at the going rate of return on capital. Any lower bid would imply a higher discount rate, or a higher profit, which would be bid away by competition. A higher bid would be unwarranted, since the profit level obtained at that bid would be below the competitive rate.

The tract evaluation technique developed in the last section stated:

$$DPV = (\text{Reserves}) (\text{New Price}) e^{-rt},$$

and as noted, a firm's bid must reflect this value. What is the

source of the wide variation of bids observed in offshore sales?
It is not realistic for a bidder to try to increase or decrease its
desired profit rate (discount rate) in a competitive situation.
Costs are roughly known and constant for a particular tract. The
future price of oil is anyone's guess, and might be one source of
variation, although there are obvious penalties for making too high
an estimate of future price. The most important source of variation
is the firm's estimate of reserves which, as will be shown, can vary
greatly. Time turns out to be another crucial variable in determining discounted present value. The sooner production can
begin on a tract, the higher its present value.

A graphic method for determining the present discounted value
of offshore leases employing the same basic technique just presented
has been developed by the U. S. Bureau of Mines. Their technique,
called nomography, uses data from the federal offshore sales to
estimate the relationship between value (represented by bid), and
the independent variables price, target discount rate and
estimated reserves.[17]

Of course, the world of offshore oil leasing sales is a far
cry from a world of perfect certainty. Uncertainty enters into
each parameter in the calculation of discounted present value, and
a risk premium, which itself is uncertain, must be figured into
the discounting factor. In the DPV equation, there are no fewer
than nine parameters which combine multiplicatively to make the
value estimate, many of them in the estimate of reserves. Each of

these parameters must be estimated by a potential bidder. When we consider that there are a number of independent bidders each making independent estimates of the parameters, the wide dispersion of bids on a tract is not so hard to understand.

Suppose a number of independent estimates of each of the parameters necessary to calculate discounted present value were available. That is, several estimates of future price, payout time, probability of finding hydrocarbons, and all of the parameters which go into the calculation of reserves, are available. If the discounted present value estimate generated by using the average value of each of these parameters, which might have been estimated by one bidder, happened to be uniformly 20 percent above the average, and there were in fact nine parameters, then the discounted present value would be $(1.2)^9 \times 100\% = 520\%$ of the DPV based on average values for each parameter. Similarly, a set of parameters which was all 20 percent below the average would produce a present value only about $(.8)^9 \times 100\% = 14\%$ of the value calculated using the average values.

Thus it is not surprising to find the wide variation in bids exhibited in Table 2-2. In the numerical example just presented, the two values differ by a factor of 37. As the number of parameters and the variance of individual parameter estimates both increase, the possible variation in final values becomes even larger.

Not only are the parameters which enter the calculation of discounted present value uncertain, but conditions within an

individual firm may influence the value which it places on a
tract. How urgently does the firm need new sources of product?
How successful has the firm been in past sales? How aggressive
are the managers of the firm? These factors and others may further
help create divergent bids for a single tract.

When a random variable is constructed as the product of a
number of other random variables, as is tract value, the resulting distribution is often lognormal. (That is, the logarithm of
the random variable is normally distributed.)[18] Thus, hydrocarbon
reserve estimates, discounted present value estimates, and bids
for offshore tracts have all been shown to be approximately lognormally distributed.[19]

Some firms use Monte Carlo simulation as an alternative technique
for evaluating offshore tracts. Rather than trying to pin down a
specific number for the value of a tract, Monte Carlo Simulation
involves estimating a probability distribution for the value.
Initially, a distribution is estimated for each parameter in the
present discounted value formula. Some of these parameters are
known with greater accuracy than others, and these differences in
knowledge are reflected in the shape and spread of the individual
distributions. When all of the parameter distributions have been
specified, a computer randomly chooses a value for each parameter,
and the value of the tract for that set of parameters is calculated.
Repetition of this process generates a frequency distribution of
possible values of the tract, and based on this overall frequency

distribution, the firm must decide what to bid. The distribution
of values generated by this method is again approximately lognormal.[20]

In making bids, firms generally follow the rule of bidding
according to present discounted value. Occasionally, however, a
firm may indulge in the game of second guessing, or may try to
pick up a bargain, or "make a steal" as it is called in the industry.
This kind of gamesmanship is particularly frequent in drainage
sales when tracts adjacent to producing tracts are offered for sale,
and information is asymmetric. A rule of thumb in the industry
states that it is risky to bid in the face of offset information
(that is, bid against another bidder who has detailed information
gained from actual drilling on an adjacent tract). For this
reason, the offsetting operator may try to sneak in a low bid
on the drainage tract. But then, a relatively low bid from
another bidder might win the tract. Such games may be fun, in a
perverse sort of way, but it is nonetheless embarrassing to out-
bid an offset operator for a drainage tract, since he has so much
more information about the value of the tract.

Some firms choose to bid a small amount on a lot of tracts
which seem to be of secondary interest, realizing that only a small
number of tracts will be won, but perhaps one will prove to be a
bargain. This behavior reflects a lack of work done in exploration,
and that deficiency will usually be paid for by having to drill
a large number of wildcat wells before finding one which pays off.
Some firms following this strategy are looking for hydrocarbons

captured in a strategraphic (strat) trap. A strat trap is unlike a salt dome anticline in that it is generally invisible to geophysical probing. Eventually bright spot technology may be useful in detecting strat traps, but at present, they are found only by chance. While they are usually quite large, they are still expensive to find. The expense is shifted, however, from the bonus payments to the wildcat drilling expenses. In general, firms rely on discounted present value estimates when constructing bids.

This section has argued that bids are lognormally distributed, and that bids reflect the estimated present discounted value of a tract. This result will be modified in Chapter III, where it will be shown that if all bidders actually bid full expected value for a tract, they would find that they were only winning those tracts on which they had overestimated the value. This problem of overbidding forms the heart of the theory in Chapter III.

Tract Development and Operation

We conclude this section on the methods of offshore exploration and development with a discussion of what happens after an offshore tract has been leased. Since the bonus payment on a tract may run to more than a hundred million dollars and is frequently in the tens of millions, development time becomes vitally important. Even a week's delay can cost many thousands of dollars in delayed returns, as pointed out'in the previous subsection.

The first step after a lease is won is to begin exploration drilling. Mobile drilling rigs are generally contracted by the tract operator from a private drilling firm, and competition to contract these rigs is fierce. Often all rigs are committed for several years in advance. It pays a firm to plan well ahead. Once a rig is in place, drilling expenses can range as high as $25,000 per day, depending on depth of water, and difficulty of drilling. The test well can take between a week and several months to complete, but a good ball park estimate for an offshore wildcat well is one million dollars. Generally, the search is not abandoned until several dry holes are drilled, since even dry holes provide useful geological information. If oil or gas is present, additional drilling confirms the size of the deposit.

If reserves are sufficient for commercial production, a permanent platform is set. A platform can typically support two or three dozen wells, and serves as a gathering point for the hydro-carbons produced. Just as with mobile rigs, drilling platforms are in short supply. Each must be specially ordered and built, and the delay may be several years. The cost of a platform again depends on the size, water depth, and weather conditions it must endure, but is on the order of five to ten million dollars.

If a tract is leased for a bonus of $50 million, wildcat drilling costs $5 million, and a platform costs $10 million, the firm faces costs of $65 million before a drop of oil has been produced or sold. That is a tremendous "front end load" to carry, and it becomes clear why time is so crucial after a sale. Some

firms find it advantageous to contract drilling rigs and order
platforms before a sale has even occurred, before they know which,
if any, tracts they will win. They reason that if they can save
time, possibly as much as a year, by having this equipment ready
when needed, it justifies the risk that it will not be needed.
Even if the firm won no tracts, the tight market for rigs and
platforms would insure their sale overnight.

3. Joint Ventures and Offshore Bidding

The costs of offshore operations are enormous, and the risks
are high. Investments on a tract can reach millions of dollars
before any return is realized, and on many tracts, no return will
ever be realized. To counter these odds, a growing number of
offshore investors are turning toward joint ventures as a way to
accumulate larger blocks of capital, and spread each individual
investor's capital over a larger number of offshore tracts.
Table 2-3 indicates the growth in popularity of joint venture
bidding over time, along with the increase in the amounts of money
involved.

As Stelzer points out, there are two sides to any joint
venture--a good side and a bad side.[21] On the one hand, joint
ventures permit projects to be carried out which might be too
expensive or too risky for a single firm to undertake. On the
other hand, however, the joining of two or more potential competitors
reduces the number of competitors. Whether the degree of competition

TABLE 2-3. STATISTICAL HISTORY OF JOINT VENTURE ACTIVITIES

| | Tracts Leased[a] | | | All Bids[b] | | |
Sale Date	Number	% Won by JV's	% of Bonus $ Spent by JV's	Number	% of Bids by JV's	% of Bonus $ Exposed by JV's
10/13/54	90	18.7%	18.4%	327	17.7%	25.2%
11/ 9/54	19	31.6	26.9	90	24.4	27.9
7/12/55	121	26.4	41.8	384	36.2	40.7
5/26/59	23	95.7	96.6	23	95.7	96.6
8/11/59	19	31.6	29.7	45	33.3	31.2
2/24/60	147	36.7	57.1	444	36.3	52.8
3/13/62	206	19.9	20.0	538	24.0	24.6
3/16/62	205	20.5	34.3	666	26.4	36.6
10/ 9/62	9	33.3	50.7	26	42.3	63.6
5/14/63	57	7.0	9.3	70	14.3	14.1
4/28/64	23	21.7	39.5	69	14.5	29.8
10/ 1/64	101	67.3	63.7	223	66.4	65.0
3/29/66	17	35.3	41.4	64	28.1	37.3
10/18/66	24	45.8	51.6	79	36.7	54.2
12/15/66	1	100.0	100.0	7	71.4	79.6
6/13/67	158	42.4	47.3	742	37.6	43.9
2/ 6/68	71	69.0	65.2	164	75.6	74.8
5/21/68	110	29.1	40.0	556	50.5	56.7
11/19/68	16	37.5	73.5	38	44.7	79.6
1/14/69	20	40.0	31.2	40	40.0	38.2
12/16/69	16	25.0	10.8	58	27.6	36.8
7/21/70	19	21.1	24.6	59	18.6	19.5
12/15/70	119	50.4	55.2	1043	46.9	54.7
11/ 4/71	11	36.4	39.4	33	36.4	41.7
9/12/72	62	67.7	69.8	324	52.2	72.9
12/19/72	116	72.4	86.2	690	78.1	83.7
6/19/73	100	90.0	97.1	551	82.4	89.2
12/20/73	87	64.4	85.1	373	62.5	76.5
3/28/74	91	72.5	75.4	402	67.9	74.8
5/29/74	102	60.8	78.0	352	59.9	72.5
7/30/74	19	52.6	58.1	57	57.9	61.2
10/16/74	136	58.8	68.3	330	56.4	65.5
2/ 4/75	113	42.5	54.2	281	52.0	61.4
5/28/75	86	51.2	51.1	191	53.4	54.0
7/29/75	66	50.0	43.2	179	54.2	47.3
12/11/75	56	42.9	79.1	166	44.6	67.3
2/18/76	34	52.9	45.2	81	49.4	53.2
4/13/76	76	59.2	90.8	244	63.1	85.4
8/17/76	93	48.4	62.5	410	65.1	74.3
11/16/76	43	65.1	85.7	117	57.3	62.2
6/23/77	124	49.2	45.7	424	55.4	61.3
10/27/77	57	47.4	47.5	142	62.0	56.0
3/28/78	43	25.6	29.5	99	16.2	24.5
4/25/78	90	55.6	55.8	283	63.3	64.5
10/31/78	35	82.9	75.4	62	88.7	82.4
12/19/78	81	44.4	47.6	288	53.8	63.8
2/28/79	39	51.3	63.6	73	56.2	57.3
6/29/79	54	55.6	86.1	112	56.3	76.5
7/31/79	81	58.0	52.0	316	63.3	69.6
All Sales	3486	47.0	66.7	12335	50.9	69.9

[a] Bonus bid tracts only (excluding royalty tracts).

[b] Including unrealistically low bids, and bids rejected by the government.

is reduced or not is a key question. In the case of bidding for
offshore oil, the question is: are there more or fewer serious
bidders in a sale, or on an average tract, as a result of allowing
joint ventures to be formed?

The Supreme Court has considered this problem on several
occasions. In U. S. vs. Terminal Railroad Association of St. Louis
(224 U.S. 383 (1912)), the Supreme Court ruled that a combination
of all railroad terminal operators in the St. Louis area was mono-
polistic, but did achieve genuine cost savings, as a result of
elimination of duplication of facilities.[22] The Court's ruling
was that the geographical circumstances in St. Louis justified a
single terminal for the group of railroads, but that the monopoly
power should not be used oppressively. To this end, the court
required that non-member railroads also be allowed to use the
terminal.

In U. S. vs. Penn-Olin Chemical Co. (378 U.S. 158 (1964)), the
Court ruled that by jointly entering the sodium chlorate market,
Pennsalt Chemicals and Olin-Mathieson Chemical reduced competition
in violation of Section 7 of the Clayton Act. The argument was
that if one of the two had entered the market alone, the other
would have been a restraining influence through its position as a
potential entrant.[23]

Kaysen and Turner hold the position that joint ventures are
useful so long as three conditions hold: first, the joint venture
does not possess market power; second, the joint venturers are not
competitors; and third, the product of the joint venture differs

from the products of the participants.[24] Joint ventures formed for
bidding for offshore oil leases fail the latter two of these
criteria. Competition does remain among different joint ventures
and single firms in the sales, however, so it is not clear that
the joint ventures possess market power through elimination of
bidding competition. This thesis will in fact investigate the
amount of market power held by bidding joint ventures, as it
affects the outcomes of offshore sales.

The Formation of Joint Ventures

Joint ventures, called partnerships or combines in the industry,
form for as many reasons as there are joint ventures themselves.
Some partnerships involve two firms, some involve fifty; they may
last for a week, or for years. The objective may be to pool money,
information, equipment, and/or risk. Some joint ventures involve
the largest oil companies in the country, some the smallest.

In short, any attempt to devise a theory of joint venture
formation and behavior is likely to be at best difficult. Nevertheless, there are certain common features of joint venture formation,
which may be included in a theory of bidding for offshore oil
leases.

Although some joint ventures are formed out of necessity, while
others are merely a convenience, partnerships do offer attractive
features to many firms. The expense and risk of leasing and developing offshore tracts, only a fraction of which are productive, make
it necessary to bid on enough tracts to be reasonably assured of

winning some productive tracts. Thus, members of a joint venture
are not only required to risk less capital on any one tract, but
they are also able to spread their limited capital over a larger
number of tracts.

Industry representatives variously describe the process of
joint venture formation as "dancing around" with potential partners,
and "getting on the phone and calling up people we think we'd
like to be with." Sometimes a desire to share or exchange information motivates a joint venture. Information motivation is
particularly strong in a drainage sale, when the land offered for
lease adjoins known producing tracts, since some bidders have
direct knowledge obtained by drilling on adjacent, previously
leased tracts. Also, as was mentioned, joint ventures may form
to pool financial and technical assets.

This section will consider five types of joint ventures:
group shoots, exploration and bidding ventures, pure bidding
ventures, investment ventures, and project ventures.[25] These
types are not mutually exclusive, but each has unique features.
The group shoot, unlike other types of joint ventures, lasts only
for a short time, dissolving long before the bidding takes place.
The other types of joint ventures form to bid on and operate
offshore tracts.

1. Group Shoots

The earliest and largest joint venture in preparation for an
offshore sale is called a group, or spec (speculative) shoot. A

group shoot acquires a fairly general body of seismic data over an area of mutual interest, for a large number of firms. Sometimes these shoots are undertaken by an independent seismic company, and sold to the industry, and sometimes they are initiated by one firm in the industry, or contracted for by a large group of firms. Each participant pays some share of the total cost, determined by the number of participants. Additional participants may subsequently purchase the data at premium rates, resulting in a partial refund to the initial contributors..

The group shoots frequently cover offshore areas which are due to come up for leasing sale in the near future, but sometimes they are on a more purely speculative basis. Group shoot activity has gone on in the Atlantic offshore since 1965, even though at that time no Atlantic sale had been scheduled.[26]

The participants in a group shoot, themselves, may be combines. There would be no purpose for members of a bidding venture already formed to independently purchase the group shoot data. The relatively low cost of this large, although admittedly incomplete, data set allows firms of all sizes to participate in the early stages of an offshore sale. The data are detailed enough to reveal major structures in the sale area, and provide enough information let firms decide which tracts warrant independent follow-up exploration.

Since March 1970, the U. S. Government has also participated in industry group shoots. Group shoot data are used to help meet the twin goals of environmental protection, and receipt of fair market value for natural resources.

2. Exploration and Bidding Joint Ventures

The group shoot does not provide sufficient data on which to base bids. At some point, prior to the sale, companies undertake own-account investigations of the tracts to be sold. Some companies investigate all tracts in the sale by themselves, some select only a few tracts for detailed analysis, while still other firms form partnerships to spread the costs of further exploration. The latter type of joint venture, designated an exploration and bidding joint venture, may be formed either before or after the group shoot.

The exploration and bidding combine generally consists of small independent firms without the expertise or the financial backing to enter an offshore leasing sale alone, and for whom it is necessary to share exploration costs as well as the bid. The problem of spreading risk is especially important to small firms. Occasionally a firm will bid all of its capital on only one or two tracts, but this is a very risky thing to do.[27] The safer strategy of spreading the risk can only be effectively done with a larger amount of capital than a single small firm commands.

The firms in exploration and bidding ventures work together for extended periods of time in one sale, and frequently the same groups of firms show up together in subsequent sales.

3. Pure Bidding Joint Ventures

Some partnerships form close to the time of a sale, perhaps as little as a week before bids are due. I designate these late forming partnerships, pure bidding joint ventures. Participants in this kind of joint venture have usually done independent analysis to evaluate the tracts offered in the sale. Members may be single firms, or they may be combines which were previously formed for the purpose of such evaluation. In particular, the major oil companies generally prefer to do their own exploration and tract evaluation, and decide whether to enter a joint venture near the time of the sale.

The major purposes of a pure bidding joint venture are to pool capital and spread risk. By their nature, these joint ventures bring together independently gathered bodies of detailed data regarding the sale tracts, and the bids submitted by these partnerships reflect this increased information. The information available to a pure bidding joint venture plays an important role in the theory of joint venture bidding developed in Chapter III. Since the independent tract value estimates of members may vary widely, as seen in Section 2, the bids submitted by a pure bidding joint venture represent the results of a negotiation concerning the correctness of each estimate. Where disagreements cannot be resolved, some members may decide not to join in bidding on all tracts. More often, however, the group submits a bid which reflects a compromise of the divergent estimates.

4. Investment Joint Ventures

Sometimes a firm outside the oil industry wishes to invest in offshore oil. Rather than enter a sale on its own, it may join an established oil company, to take advantage of that company's

expertise in the field of offshore exploration. One recent
example of this behavior has been the Northwest Mutual Life
Insurance Company, which has bid with Amoco in several sales.
In exchange for the oil company's knowledge, and willingness to
handle all of the exploration, bidding and production, the invest-
ing company pays a premium by bearing a larger share of the costs
than it receives of revenues. This kind of joint venture is not
very common.

5. Joint Venture to Guarantee Product

Several types of joint ventures are included under this
heading. The most common involves natural gas utility companies.
Due to the regulation of the price of natural gas, any company
discovering gas and wishing to sell it has the price set for it.
Gas companies, however, need product to uphold their utility
charters, and frequently the regulated market price of natural
gas is below the internal value of the gas to the utility. Faced
with the choice of obtaining natural gas or losing their charter,
utilities are frequently willing to buy into offshore joint ventures
at a premium, just to "get a call on" (be guaranteed of) any
natural gas which is discovered.

Another type of partnership which falls into this category
forms between oil companies, and the owners of drilling rigs, or
builders of platforms. Such a joint venture insures the oil firms
of a source of rigs and platforms, and the contractors of buyers
for their equipment. It would seem that the contractors could

demand a premium, due to the great demand for their products.

A Note on Post-Sale Transactions

A word about post-sale transactions concludes this section on the formation of joint ventures. Some firms prefer not to go through the difficulty and expense of offshore leasing sales, but still want to be a part of offshore operations. These firms seek to enter into joint ventures with successful bidders after a sale. These firms must pay a premium for the risk and expense undertaken by the successful bidder.

A firm buying an interest in offshore tracts after a sale, has not always planned to follow this strategy. Bidders are occasionally shut out of a sale, winning few, or none of the tracts on which they bid. When this happens, unsuccessful bidders may inquire whether any winners are willing to sell an interest in any of their tracts. Similarly, by fate or design, one bidder may incur a greater financial burden in a sale than it wishes to carry. To reach a more comfortable level of investment, the over-committed firm will happily sell interests in the tracts which it has bought. Not surprisingly, these two situations frequently go hand in hand: when some bidders have been shut out in a sale, some other bidders find that they have bought more than they expected.[28]

Provisions of Joint Venture Contracts

Joint ventures are legal agreements among individual firms, to carry out certain specified activities. The activities specified in offshore oil joint ventures include exploration, bidding, development and production on offshore tracts. The previous section described the exploration and bidding arrangements of different types of joint ventures. Usually a joint venture contract assigns one member as the principal operator. Should a tract be won, the principal operator is in charge of developing and producing any hydrocarbons present. Sometimes the principal operating firm handles the work itself, but more often, tasks are contracted to specialized firms.

The joint venture agreement of course specifies how costs and revenues are to be shared by the member firms. Some members may receive a higher share of the revenue than they pay in costs, if they contribute to the project in other ways, such as providing specialized knowledge or equipment.

The handling of partners who do not wish to bid on certain tracts, or who wish to drop out of a joint venture completely, presents a particularly interesting problem in writing joint venture agreements. The agreements must be carefully worded so that they are not attacked as anti-competitive by either the Interior or Justice Departments. On one hand, drop-outs should not be banned from bidding altogether, but on the other hand, once a firm obtains information from one set of partners, it should not be allowed to join a new joint venture.

This problem is handled by what is called a "back-out, back-in" provision, found in most joint venture contracts. This clause states that any firm can leave (back out of) a partnership at any time, for any reason. Reasons might include unwillingness to bid at the level other members want to bid, the desire to participate in only a few tracts from financial necessity, or a desire to bid alone on some tracts. A firm may not, however, join any other partnership after dropping out of one joint venture. If, at a future date, the firm wishes to rejoin the group, it may buy back its original share of the project.

The back-in clause holds even if a single member of the venture decides to bid alone for a tract, in competition with its own joint venture. Such a case occurred in the March 1974 sale, as reported by the Wall Street Journal:

> The Chevron unit itself made one of the more unusual bids of the sale. Together with nine partners, it offered $4,454,300 for a 2,500-acre tract in the West Cameron area a few miles off the Louisiana Coast. Then, acting alone, Chevron strangely made a higher and apparently winning bid of $4,638,000 for the same tract.
>
> A company spokesman later explained Chevron made the second bid on its own after hearing a rumor that "confidential information" about the first offer had "leaked out" before the sale. The higher bid was submitted "as a hedge" against a possible competitive offer--which never materialized--that might have been made on the basis of the rumored leak, the spokesman indicated. He said Chevron's partners in the initial bid would have the option to acquire interests in the higher offer.[29]

Another type of arrangement occasionally employed after a sale, is a farmout. A farmout turns the operation of a lease over to an outside firm or combine. Terms of farmouts vary. The original lease holders may retain a partial interest in the tract, or not. Farmouts were originally a common way for small independent firms to participate in offshore operations. Larger firms were willing to farm out marginal tracts which they were too busy to explore, or which they had already explored and discarded. Now that bidding joint ventures provide a more common way for small firms to enter the offshore oil industry, farmouts are less important.

FOOTNOTES

1. L. K. Weaver, C. J. Jirik and H. F. Pierce, Offshore
Petroleum Studies: Historical and Estimated Future
Hydrocarbon Production from U. S. Offshore Areas and the
Impact on the Onshore Segment of the Petroleum Industry.
(Information Circular 8575) (Washington: U. S. Department
of Interior, Bureau of Mines, 1973), p. 1.

2. "Offshore Oil Leasing will Surge in the 1970's, Interior
Chief Says," The Wall Street Journal, January 23, 1974, p. 4.

3. The interviews, conducted in the fall of 1973, were with
representatives of three major and three independent oil
companies, all of which have actively participated in offshore leasing sales. The companies will remain anonymous.
Information was also gathered from Mr. John Rankin,
Director of the O.C.S. Office of the Bureau of Land
Management in New Orleans; Mr. J. Rogers Pearcy of the U. S.
Geological Survey also in New Orleans; and Mr. Uriel Dutton,
of the law firm of Fulbright and Drooker, in Houston, Texas.

4. This section draws on Keith Brown, Bidding for Offshore Oil:
Toward an Optimal Strategy. (Dallas: Southern Methodist
University Press, 1969), pp. 26-28. For a legislative history
of federal offshore leasing activity, see the statement of
Dr. Frank J. Barry contained in U. S. Congress, Senate,
Committee on the Judiciary Subcommittee on Antitrust and
Monopoly, Governmental Intervention in the Market Mechanism
The Petroleum Industry, Part 5: Federally Owned Oil and
Gas Lands on the Outer Continental Shelf. (91st Congress,
2nd session, August 11 and 13, 1970, pursuant to Senate
Resolution 40) (Washington: Government Printing Office,
1970), pp. 1907-1912. (Hereinafter referred to as Senate
Hearings on Offshore Oil) Additional legislative background
is in Lowell G. Hammons, "Subsea Seismic Survey Data Aid
Federal Government in Deep Water Leasing in U. S.," Offshore,
Vol. 33, No. 6 (June 5, 1973), pp. 29 ff.

5. "Drilling News," Offshore, Vol. 35, No. 1 (January, 1975), p. 5.
More recently, Exxon, Mobil and Union announced that they
planned to abandon six tracts off the coast of Florida,
after drilling a seventh dry hole. Total bonus paid for
the six track was $632 million, including the $212 million
for one of the six. "Exxon Group Hints it May Have Ended
Oil Hunt Off Florida," The Wall Street Journal, June 11, 1975,
p. 4.

6. Lowell G. Hammons, op. cit., p. 30.

7. Senate Hearings on Offshore Oil, op. cit., p. 30.

8. The O.C.S. Office in New Orleans has released a memorandum, dated November, 1974, entitled "Proposed O.C.S. Planning Schedule," showing the increased time allowed for environmental considerations.

9. Memo from Charles Schultz, Director, Bureau of the Budget. to Stewart Udall, Secretary of the Interior, November 20, 1967; reprinted in Senate Committee Hearings, op. cit., pp. 2082, 2083.

10. Lowell G. Hammons, op. cit., p. 29.

11. "Interior Agency to Regulate the Disclosure of Data Collected on Offshore U. S. Tracts," The Wall Street Journal, May 16, 1974, p. 10.

12. "Offshore Leasing Gamble--Pay Your Money and Take Your Chances," Offshore, Vol. 32, No. 8 (July, 1972), p. 35.

13. "U. S. Rejects 23 of 114 High Bids in Oil Lease Sale," The Wall Street Journal, April 10, 1972, p. 2.

14. James C. Tanner, "'Bright Spot'--New Technique Used to Find Oil and Gas Before Drilling Wells," The Wall Street Journal, May 22, 1974, p. 1.

15. This presentation is adapted from Paul B. Crawford, "Texas Offshore Bidding Patterns," Journal of Petroleum Technology, Vol. 22 (March, 1970), pp. 283-289.

16. In continuous time, the problem becomes:

$$DPV = \int_{t_0}^{T} [\text{Production (t)} \times \text{Price (t)} - \text{Cost (t)}]\, e^{-rt}\, dt;$$

where t_0 = initial time,

T = time at which reserves are fully produced.

See also T. M. Garland, W. D. Dietzman and J. G. Thompson, Determining Discounted Cash Flow Rate of Return and Payout Time for Onshore Development Wells. (Information Circular 8593) (Washington: U. S. Department of Interior, Bureau of Mines, 1973).

17. L. K. Weaver, H. F. Pierce and C. J. Jirik, Nomograph for Estimating Hydrocarbon Lease Bonus Bids in the Gulf of Mexico. (Information Circular 8609) (Washington: U. S. Department of Interior, Bureau of Mines, 1973).

18. "...The Lognormal is a fundamental distribution in statistics, as is the normal... It arises from a theory of elementary errors combined by a multiplicative process, just as the normal distribution arises from a theory of elementary errors combined by addition." J. Aitchison and J. A. C. Brown, The Lognormal Distribution, quoted in Gordon M. Kaufman, Statistical Decision and Related Techniques in Oil and Gas Exploration. (Englewood Cliffs, N. J.: Prentice Hall, 1963), p. 109.

19. For a discussion of the lognormal distribution as it relates to oil and gas exploration, see Gordon Kauffman, op. cit., pp. 101-126. The lognormal distribution as it applies to bidding is discussed in John J. Arps, "A Strategy for Sealed Bidding," Journal of Petroleum Technology, Vol. 17 (September, 1965), p. 1036; Paul B. Drawford, loc. cit., and Keith Brown, op. cit., pp. 35-39.

20. Interview with J. Rogers Pearcy, U. S. Geological Survey, Metarie, Louisiana, November, 1973.

21. Irwin M. Stelzer, Selected Antitrust Cases: Landmark Decisions. (4th ed; Homewood, Ill: Richard D. Irwin, 1972), p. 226.

22. A. D. Neale, The Antitrust Laws of the United States. (2nd ed; Cambridge: The University Press, 1970), p. 127.

23. Ibid, p. 198.

24. C. Kaysen and F. Turner, Antitrust Policy: An Economic and Legal Analysis (Cambridge: Harvard University Press, 1959) pp. 136 ff; summarized in Neale, loc. cit.

25. This classification is my own, based on interviews with sale participants, and an examination of the historical pattern of joint venture bidding.

26. "Geophysical Program to Resume in Atlantic," Offshore, Vol. 32, No. 8 (July, 1972), p. 78.

27. For example, in the October, 1954 sale, Forest Oil Co. bid a total of $6,585,000 on six tracts. It won one of the tracts with a bid of $6,100,000, and lost the other five, over which it had spread the remaining $485,000.

28. A complete record of all post-sale transactions is contained in the Serial Register, a document available for public inspection at the Outer Continental Shelf Office of the Bureau of Land Management in New Orleans. The Serial Register lists the current ownership of each offshore lease, and the firm designated as operator of each tract.

29. "Offshore Louisiana Oil, Gas Lease Sale Nearly Doubled Usual Number of Bidders," The Wall Street Journal, April 1, 1974, p. 12.

CHAPTER III

A THEORY OF OFFSHORE BIDDING

1. A Review of the Bidding Literature[1]

The literature on competitive bidding can be divided into two
categories: theoretical and applied. The first approach treats
an auction as an N-person non-cooperative game. The equilibrium
in a bidding game occurs when each player has chosen a strategy
which maximizes his expected payoff, subject to the strategies
chosen by his opponents. Such an equilibrium is called a Nash
equilibrium. Christianson has summarized the game theoretic
approach to bidding:

> It is assumed that one's opponents are rational decision
> makers who seek to maximize a known payoff function.
> This assumption is used to predict how these opponents
> will behave.[2]

The applied bidding literature develops a theory of decision
making under uncertainty. The uncertain factors include not only
the value of the objects for sale, but also the behavior of
opponents. Several authors include the use of conditional
probabilities, so that a player's expectations about the future
are conditioned by past events. Use of such conditioned expectations
is called Bayesian decision theory.

Theoretical Literature

The game theory approach to competitive bidding attempts to
characterize equilibrium solutions. In order to reach these results,

it must be assumed that each player has a payoff function which is known by all. For practical purposes, however, bidding games in which all payoff functions are fixed, and known by all players, are not particularly interesting.

> Sealed bidding when the individuals have known fixed costs and known valuations presents both an institutionally and mathematically uninspiring problem. The noncooperative equilibrium point will award the contract to the individual with the lowest cost (or equivalently the highest valuation for an item) at a price just under that of the individual with the next higher cost. ...

> In industry, auctions, sales, and all economic activities which use sealed bids or other auctioning devices, the problems which call for analysis appear to arise from considerations such as capacity constraints, sequential choices in dynamic markets, and, above all, lack of knowledge of the costs and valuations of others, and possibly a lack of knowledge of one's own costs and valuations. [3]

The lack of knowledge of costs and valuations proves to be of utmost importance in discussing bidding for offshore oil. In their important four part work on bidding processes, Griesmer, Levitan and Shubik[4] begin by using the assumption of perfect knowledge, but in part IV relax that assumption. Part IV of their work extends an article by Vickery,[5] dealing with bidding situations where costs and valuations of each bidder are drawn from known probability distributions. Vickery treats a variety of different types of auction sales, including sealed bidding, while Griesmer, et.al. concentrate on sealed bidding sales.

The Nash equilibrium conditions examined by both Vickery and Griesmer, et.al., involve computation of a Cournot-type reaction function for each bidder, which indicates what bid will maximize expected value, given a set of opponents' bids. The equilibrium is characterized by the fact that in the face of opponents bidding their equilibrium values, a bidder maximizes his expected payoff by bidding his own equilibrium value.

In offshore oil sales, different bidders have different amounts of information, and place varying degrees of confidence in that information. This problem of asymmetry is treated in both Vickery and Griesmer, et.al., by making the assumption that the probability distributions from which values are drawn are not identical for all bidders. Robert Wilson[6] presents a special case of asymmetric information, in which one bidder has perfect knowledge of the value of the object for sale, while other bidders face uncertainty.[7] Wilson cites as an example of this extreme case of asymmetry, an offshore drainage sale in which one bidder already owns tracts adjacent to the tract offered for sale, and has nearly perfect knowledge of the value of the sale tract. Other bidders lack this knowledge, and face uncertainty.[8] Wilson concludes that a bidder with better information maximizes his expected payoff with a bid less than the (known, to him) value of the tract. Wilson has also shown that the results are not qualitatively different if no bidder has perfect knowledge, but knowledge is asymmetric.[9]

In both symmetric and asymmetric information cases, the game theoretic models suggest a Nash equilibrium in which each player's optimal strategy (bid) depends on the strategies (bids) of all other players. The remaining sections of this chapter develop a similar model of competitive bidding with a Nash equilibrium.

The model incorporates certain problems of competitive bidding brought out by the applied bidding literature, as well as some particular features of offshore leasing sales.

Applied Literature

The applied bidding literature, rather than characterizing equilibrium conditions, deals with some of the practical problems facing a competitive bidder. The applied literature views the auction sale from a single bidder's point of view, and suggests methods for making successful (profitable) bids.

The problem facing a participant in a sealed bid auction can be expressed in a model of expected profit maximization:

$$\pi(B) = (V - B) \, P(B);$$

where
$\pi(B)$ is expected profit,

V is expected gross value of winning,

B is bid level,

$V-B$ is expected net value of winning,

$P(B)$ is the probability that bid B wins.

Maximizing with respect to bid level B gives a condition which equates the expected marginal revenue with the expected marginal cost:

$$\frac{d\pi}{dB} = (V - B) \, P'(B) - 1 \cdot P(B) = 0$$

$$V \, P'(B) = B \, P'(B) + P(B)$$

(Expected Marginal Revenue) = (Expected Marginal Cost)

Keith Brown employs this model in his book, _Bidding for Offshore Oil_.[10] In that work, Brown develops a formula:

> ...for calculating the expected profit maximizing bid as a function of the expected value of the tract, the predicted standard deviation of the bids of competitors, and the estimated number of competing bidders.[11]

Brown's book discusses many of the problems encountered by an offshore bidder. Of course, tract value must be estimated. But to know the probability of winning with a bid B, a bidder must know something about the number of competitors, and how they are likely to bid.

Hanssmann and Rivett consider the problem of "making simultaneous bids for a number of objects against competition by an unknown number of competitors."[12] Their work extends a Ph.D. dissertation by Lawrence Friedman on the same subject.[13] Hanssmann and Rivett wish to determine the probability that a bidder will simultaneously defeat N opponents with a bid of B. If the probability of defeating the ith opponent is $P_i(B)$, and all bids are submitted independently, then the probability of winning (defeating all N opponents) is

$$\prod_{i=1}^{N} P_i(B).$$

If in addition, all of the P_i are the same, the probability of winning reduces to $[P(B)]^N$. In order to estimate N, the number of opponents, Hanssmann and Rivett derive a positive relationship between estimated tract value, V, and the expected number of opponents, N.

Brown suggests that one problem arising in offshore bidding is the constraint on bids forced by a financial constraint.[14] John J. Arps, in "A Strategy for Sealed Bidding,"[15] employs such a capital constraint. Arps assumes that firms wish to maximize the number of tracts leased, subject to constraints on tract profitability and capital bid. In his analysis, a target rate of return is included in the calculations of the expected range of bids on a tract. The selection of a target rate of return, rather than an attempt to maximize profits, seems more consistant with reported industry practice.[16]

The Overbidding Problem

One major difficulty with the bidding literature, both theoretical and applied, is the inherent bias in the evaluation of objects won by a bidder. Most of the models discussed assume that bidders maximize expected payoff. Several authors have pointed out however, that because bidders win those objects which they valued most optimistically, the estimated values of objects won are not unbiased. Hence, bidders' actual payoffs consistently fall short of their expectations. Keith Brown has stated the problem as follows:

> ... The profit to the winner will be the difference
> between the actual value and the amount bid. Since
> each firm makes a bid based at least in part on
> value estimate, the larger the value estimate with
> respect to the true value, ceteris paribus, the
> higher the bid the firm makes, the more likely it
> becomes that the firm's bid will win, and the small-
> er the firm's actual profit will be if it does win.[17]

Brown has argued that although overall tract evaluation is unbiased, evaluation of objects which are won is not unbiased, and in fact the objects which are won tend to be those which were valued too highly.

Brown's argument is presented in response to the general problem of choosing among alternative investments of uncertain value. The same conclusions have been independently reached, in slightly more detailed form, for the specific problem of bidding in offshore leasing sales, by Capen, Clapp and Campbell.[18] Their conclusion is summed up in one sentence. "In competitive bidding, the winner tends to be the player who most overestimates true tract value."[19]

This problem of biased evaluations of tracts won will be designated the overbidding problem. The bidding model to be developed will include an allowance for the overbidding problem, so that payoffs to winners do not consistently fall short of their expectations.

Section 2 of this chapter develops a model of bidding in which all participants are identical in all respects. Section 3 relaxes this assumption, allowing some bidders to be able to more accurately estimate the value of tracts. Section 4 interprets joint ventures as bidders with more accurate information, in the sense developed in section 3. Finally, a set of hypotheses concerning joint ventures is stated in section 5.

2. An Auction with Identical Bidders

Consider initially that a single firm wishes to bid on a tract in an offshore leasing sale. Further, suppose that the firm has estimated a value of the tract, as discussed in Chapter II, section 2. Recall the many variables which go into an estimation of tract value--estimated reserves, prices and costs, target rate of return, to name a few. The firm must realize that its estimate is just that, an estimate, and is subject to error. We might write:

(1) $$V = V* \cdot U$$

where V is the estimated value of the tract; V* is the true worth of the tract, calculated hypothetically using the true (but unknown) values of all of the parameters in the present discounted value equation of Chapter II; and U is a lognormally distributed random disturbance term. The disturbance term enters multiplicatively, and is lognormally distributed since estimated tract value is calculated as the product of several random variables. Taking the natural logarithm of equation 1 yields:

(2) $$\ell n(V) = \ell n(V*) + \ell n(U),$$

and letting lower case letters stand for natural logarithms:

(3) $$v = v* + u.$$

The random variable u is normally distributed, as is v. A rational firm would like its estimate of v* (and thus of V* also) to be unbiased. On some tracts, the estimate v would be too large, and on other tracts the estimate would be too small, but on average, v would equal v*. Unbiased estimation means that:

(4) $\qquad E(v) = v*$, or

(5) $\qquad E(u) = 0$.

Suppose that a firm places a bid which equals its estimate of the tract value. Several firms claim that they do bid by this method, as discussed in Chapter II. A firm using this strategy faces exactly the problem of overbidding discussed by Brown, and Capen, et. al.[20] In competition with bidders employing the same strategy, the estimated values of tracts which a bidder actually wins are not unbiased. Specifically, each bidder tends to win tracts on which the random error term, u is positive. Recall the conclusion voiced by Capen, et. al.: "In competitive bidding, the winner tends to be the player who most overestimates true tract value."[21]

The theory of order statistics helps to explain the over-bidding problem. The ith order statistic is by definition the ith largest observation in a random sample. The median of a distribution-- the middle observation in a sample--is probably the best known order statistic. In bidding theory, the first order statistic (largest observation) is of particular interest. The literature on order statistics derives actual distributions of various order statistics.[22]

The distribution of an order statistic depends on both the distribution $p(x)$ from which the sample has been drawn, and the sample size, N. The exact distribution of the ith order statistic, denoted $h^i(x)$, is expressed as:

(6) $\qquad h^i(x) = \dfrac{N!}{(i-1)!(N-i)!} \, [P(x)]^{N-i} \, [1 - P(x)]^{i-1} \, p(x),$

where $P(x)$ is the cumulative distribution function associated with $p(x)$.[23] The distribution $h^i(x)$ expresses the probability that a particular random variable x exceeds exactly $N-i$ other random variables in a sample of size N from $p(x)$, and x is also smaller than the remaining $i-1$ variables in the sample. The first order statistic is found by letting $i = 1$:

(7) $\qquad h^1(x) = N \, [P(x)]^{N-1} p(x),$

and gives the probability that x exceeds every other element of the sample.

Another interpretation of the first order statistic is that $h^1(x)$ gives the probability distribution of a random variable x conditioned on the fact that it is the largest element in a random sample of size N:

(8) $\qquad h^1(x) = \text{Prob}(x | x \text{ is largest in sample})$

$$= \frac{\text{Prob (x \underline{and} x is largest)}}{\text{Prob (x is largest)}}$$

$$= \frac{p(x) \cdot [P(x)]^{N-1}}{\displaystyle\int_{-\infty}^{\infty} [P(x)]^{N-1} \, p(x) \, dx} \, .$$

But the denominator simplifies as follows:

$$(9) \quad \int_{-\infty}^{\infty} [P(x)]^{N-1} \, p(x) \, dx = \int_{-\infty}^{\infty} [P(x)]^{N-1} \, dP(x)$$

$$= \frac{1}{N} [P(x)]^{N} \Big|_{-\infty}^{\infty}$$

$$= \frac{1}{N} [1 - 0]^{N}$$

$$= \frac{1}{N},$$

which again shows that:

$$(10) \quad h^1(x) = \text{Prob}(x \mid x \text{ is largest in sample})$$
$$= N[P(x)]^{N-1} \, p(x).$$

Returning to the overbidding problem, the theory of order statistics permits an estimate of the degree to which winning bids exceed true tract value. Suppose that N identical firms each evaluate an offshore tract in the manner discussed in Chapter II, and denote those estimates by V_1, V_2, ..., V_N. The assumption of identical firms means that each firm can be treated as drawing its estimate of value from the same (lognormal) probability distribution. This assumption means not only that each firm uses the same evaluation techniques, but also that the true worth of the tract to each firm is the same, V*. If each firm knew the true values for such parameters as hydrocarbon reserves and future prices and costs, they would place the same value on the tract. Thus V*, although unknown, is independent of the bidder making the evaluation, and is equal for all bidders. The vector $(V_1, ..., V_N)$ represents a random sample of size N from a lognormal distribution. Taking logarithms, $(v_1, \ldots, v_N)$ is a random sample of size N from the associated normal distribution, denoted by $p(v)$.

If all firms place bids equal to their respective estimates of tract value, then the vector of bids $(B_1, \ldots, B_n)$ also represents a sample of size N from the same lognormal distribution, and the logarithms of those bids, $(b_1, \ldots, b_N)$ are again a sample from the associated normal distribution.

Since the evaluation techniques used by firms are unbiased, the mean of the lognormal distribution from which values are drawn must equal the true value of the tract, V*. The mean of the associated normal distribution is then $\ell n V^* = v^*$. Table 3-1 presents the first and second moments of the distributions of the first order statistic (winning bid) for several values of N, assuming that the sample is drawn from a standard normal distribution (that is, a normal distribution with zero mean and unit standard deviation). For any number of bidders greater than one, the mean winning bid (mean first order statistic) exceeds the population mean, v^*. Figure 3-1 shows the case of five bidders, when $b_1, \ldots, b_5$ are drawn from a standard normal distribution ($v^* = 0$).

Consider the plight of the ith bidder. By placing bids which equal unbiased estimates of the true tract value, Figure 3-1 shows that the expected error in evaluation of those tracts which were won, is 1.16. Another way of expressing the overbidding problem is to say that the expected bid, b_1, conditioned on the fact that

TABLE 3-1

Moments of the Distribution of the First Order Statistic for Samples
of Size N Drawn from a Standard Normal Population

N	Mean	Standard Deviation
1	.000	1.000
2	.564	.826
5	1.163	.669
10	1.539	.587
20	1.867	.525
60	2.319	.454
100	2.508	.429

Note: As N increases, the distribution of the order statistic
diverges more and more from the normal.

Source: Tippett (1925).

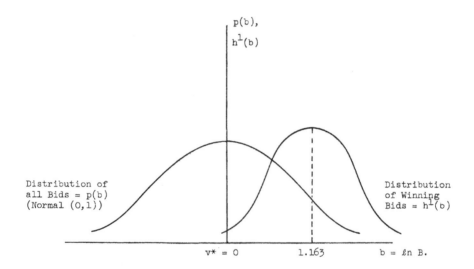

Figure 3-1.   Distribution of all bids and of winning bid, showing

the Overbidding Problem.

the ith bidder wins, does not equal v*. For the case shown in Figure 3-1:

$$(11) \qquad E(b_i | i \text{ wins}) = v* + 1.16$$

If the ith firm realized its tendency to overbid, it might adopt a new bidding strategy, in which its bid was somewhat less than its estimate of value. In a practical sense, a firm would learn how to bid over a period of time. Initially, a firm which bid its estimate of a tract's worth would discover that tracts which it won turned out to be worth less than the estimated value. The firm would gradually reduce its bids in future sales, until it was on average paying what tracts were worth. Specifically, suppose:

$$(12) \qquad B_i = \frac{V_i}{K_i} ;$$

or, taking logarithms:

$$(13) \qquad b_i = v_i - k_i.$$

Firm i wishes to choose k_i so that:

$$(14) \qquad E(b_i | i \text{ wins}) \leq v*.$$

Under the Cournot assumption that all other bidders bid their full estimate of a tract's value, firm i can calculate its minimum k_i by solving the following equation for k_i.

$$(15) \qquad E(b_i | i \text{ wins}) = v*;$$

where:

$$(16) \quad E(b_i \mid i \text{ wins}) \equiv \int_{-\infty}^{\infty} b_i \cdot \text{Prob}(b_i \mid i \text{ wins}) \, db_i$$

$$= \int_{-\infty}^{\infty} (v_i - k_i) \; \frac{[P(v_i - k_i)]^{N-1} \, p(v_i)}{\{ \int_{-\infty}^{\infty} [P(v_i - k_i)]^{N-1} p(v_i) dv_i \}} \; dv_i.$$

Equation 16 seems quite complicated, but note the similarity between $\text{Prob}(b_i \mid i \text{ wins})$, and $h^1(x)$ given by equation 8. Equation 16 cannot be directly solved for k_i except in special cases. In general, numerical methods must be used.[24] As k_i increases from zero, the expected winning bid by the ith firm decreases, and the solution to equation 15 gives the value for k_i which would prevent any overbidding, on average. Of course if the ith firm is the only firm correcting for the overbidding problem, its probability of winning falls along with its expected winning bid. If all firms make equal corrections for overbidding, then the ith firm's probability of winning is unchanged.

The final consideration of this section is the case in which all bidders do correct for the overbidding problem. Not only does each firm make an estimate of tract value, v_j, but each firm also chooses a correction factor, k_j, so that:

$$(17) \quad b_j = v_j - k_j, \quad j = 1, \ldots, N.$$

The correct choice of k_i by the ith firm now depends on all of the other k_j. Firm i would choose that k_i which satisfies equation 15, where now:

$$(18) \quad E(b_i | i \text{ wins}) = \int_{-\infty}^{\infty} (v_i - k_i) \quad \frac{\displaystyle\prod_{\substack{j=1 \\ j \neq i}}^{N} P(v_i - k_i + k_j) \, p(v_i)}{\left\{ \displaystyle\int_{-\infty}^{\infty} \prod_{\substack{j=1 \\ j \neq i}}^{N} P(v_i - k_i + k_j) \, p(v_i) \, dv_i \right\}} \, dv_i.$$

The solution to equation 15 can be written in the form of a reaction function:

$$(19) \qquad k_i = \psi_i(k_1, \ \ldots, \ k_{i-1}, \ k_{i+1}, \ \ldots, \ k_N).$$

The set of all such reaction functions will determine a Nash equilibrium set of strategies. Figure 3-2 graphs the reaction functions for the case $N = 2$, and $p(v) = 1$ on the interval $[0,1]$. At the equilibrium, $k_1 = k_2 = 1/6$, each firm expects to win with a bid of $1/2$, which equals the true tract value, v^*.

The reaction functions when $p(v)$ is a normal distribution must in general be approximated by numerical methods. In the case of identical bidders however, when all k_j are equal, it is easy to see that the expected winning bid is reduced by the amount k_j. For the ith firm:

$$(20) \qquad E(b_i | i \text{ wins}) = E(v_i - k_i | i \text{ wins})$$

$$= E(v_i | i \text{ wins}) - k_i.$$

But in the case of all k_j equal, $E(v_i | i \text{ wins})$ is simply the expected value of the first order statistic of a sample of size N drawn from $p(v)$. For the conditions of Figure 3-1 with $N = 5$, and $p(v)$ standard normal,

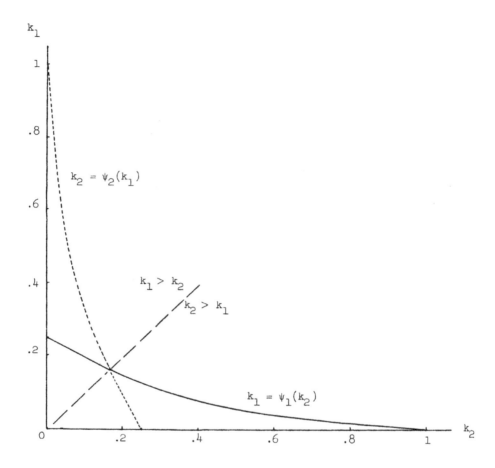

Figure 3-2. Bidding reaction functions; Symmetric Case, N = 2,
$p(v) = 1$ on $[0,1]$.

Note: ψ_1 is defined as follows: $k_1 = \frac{1}{4} - \frac{1}{2} k_2$, for $k_1 \geq k_2$;

$$k_1 = \frac{1 - \frac{1}{3} x^2}{2 - x^2} - \frac{1}{2}, \text{ where } x = 1 - k_2 + k_1, \text{ for } k_1 < k_2.$$

(21) $E(v_i | i \text{ wins}) = 1.16$, and

(22) $E(b_i | i \text{ wins}) = 1.16 - k_i$.

Since $v^* = 0$, the optimal k_i is 1.16, so long as all other bidders
are using $k_j = 1.16$. Thus, for the case of N identical bidders,
the Nash equilibrium occurs when each firm chooses k_j equal to the
expected largest value of the random sample of all value estimates,
$(v_1, \ldots, v_N)$. Figure 3-3 shows how the distribution from which
a firm chooses its bid compares to the distribution of its value
estimate, for the case N = 5, p(v) is standard normal, and
$k_j = 1.16$ for j = 1, ..., 5.

3. An Auction with Asymmetric Information

The previous section discussed a bidding model in which
identical firms adjusted their bids in order to deal with the overbidding problem. The results of that model are summarized in the
following quotation:

> The bidding model gives us a bid that we can make with
> confidence, and be happy with when we win. Yes, we may
> have over-estimated value. But we bid lower than our
> value estimate--hedging against expected error. In a
> probability sense, we "guarantee" that we obtain the
> rate of return we want.[25]

This section relaxes the assumption of identical bidders.
Suppose now that each bidder draws its estimate of tract value
from a different probability distribution, denoted $p_i(v)$,
i = 1, ..., N, where N is the number of bidders. All estimates

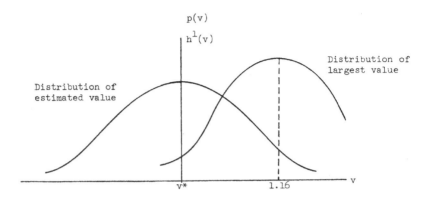

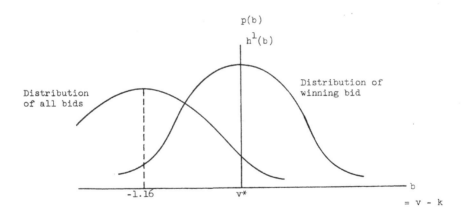

Figure 3-3. Distribution of estimated value (top) and bid (bottom)
with distribution of the corresponding first order
statistic. N = 5, p(v) is standard normal.

are still unbiased, so that each $p_i(V)$ has the same mean, V*, equal
to the true (unknown) value of the tract. As mentioned in the
previous section, this assumption means that although firms may
possess different amounts of information about a tract, if they
actually knew the value of parameters describing the tract, they
would calculate equal values for the tract.

The differences in information among bidders should be interpreted as varying abilities to forecast the true value of a tract.
Bidders with better information select their value estimate from
a narrower range than other bidders. The next section will argue
that certain types of joint ventures are able to gather more
accurate information for use in tract evaluation.

Since each firm's estimate of tract value is drawn from a
different distribution, the evaluations made of a tract by N
different firms no longer forms a sample drawn from a single
probability distribution. Rather, each observation V_i is drawn
from a different distribution, $p_i(V)$. The pure theory of order
statistics no longer applies, but the problem of estimating the
winning bid in this case is analogous to using order statistics.
Firms must still determine the extent to which they will overbid
if they bid their full estimate of tract value.

The distribution of a "modified first order statistic" differs
from bidder to bidder. For the ith bidder, the distribution of a
winning bid, given that all bidders (including the ith) bid their
estimate of a tract's value, is:

$$(23) \quad h_i^1(V_i) = \text{Prob}(V_i | i \text{ wins})$$

$$= \frac{\text{Prob}(V_i \text{ and } i \text{ wins})}{\text{Prob}(i \text{ wins})}$$

$$= \frac{p_i(V_i) \cdot \displaystyle\prod_{\substack{j=1 \\ j \neq i}}^{N} P_j(V_i)}{\displaystyle\int_{-\infty}^{\infty} p_i(V_i) \cdot \displaystyle\prod_{\substack{j=1 \\ j \neq i}}^{N} P_j(V_i) dV_i}$$

where $P_j(V)$ represents the cumulative distributions associated with the $p_j(V)$. Equation 23 is a direct extention of the distribution of a first order statistic given by equation 8. The mean of the distribution of winning bids in equation 23 is:

$$(24) \quad E(V_i | i \text{ wins}) = \int_{-\infty}^{\infty} V_i \, h_i^1(V_i) \, dV_i.$$

Although there are no tables compiled for finding the distribution of this so-called modified first order statistic, the overbidding problem still exists. Bidder i can still calculate theoretically what fraction K_i of its value estimate to bid in order to pay on average the correct (true) value for tracts which it wins.

To analyze the overbidding problem in the asymmetric case, consider again logarithms of value estimates, v_i, and suppose bidders construct bids according to equation 13:

$$(13) \quad b_i = v_i - k_i.$$

Recall that for the ith bidder to expect to pay only v* for tracts which he wins, k_i should be selected so that:

(15) $E(b_i | i \text{ wins}) = v*.$

But the calculation of $E(b_i | i \text{ wins})$ now requires use of the modified first order statistic concept. Consider the general case where all bidders are adopting strategies to combat the overbidding problem, so values for the k_j, $j = 1, \ldots, N$ are non-zero. The expression for $E(b_i | i \text{ wins})$ becomes:

(25)

$$E(b_i | i \text{ wins}) = \int_{-\infty}^{\infty} b_i \ \text{Prob}(b_i | i \text{ wins}) \ db_i$$

$$= \int_{-\infty}^{\infty} (v_i - k_i) \ \frac{\prod_{\substack{j=1 \\ j \neq i}}^{N} P_j(v_i - k_i + k_j) \cdot p_i(v_i)}{[\int_{-\infty}^{\infty} \prod_{\substack{j=1 \\ i \neq j}}^{N} P_j(v_i - k_i + k_j) \cdot p_i(v_i) \ dv_i]} \ dv_i \cdot$$

Setting equation 25 equal to $v*$ allows k_i to be calculated as a function of the values of the k_j, $j \neq i$. The equilibrium values for the k_j cannot be easily computed, for they will not all be equal. There will still be a set of N reaction functions of the form of equation 19, however, and the Nash equilibrium is the vector $(k_1, \ldots, k_N)$ which satisfies all of the reaction functions.

To investigate the properties of the equilibrium where bidders have asymmetric information, two techniques were employed: a numerical example, and a computer simulation. The numerical example involves two firms, one which choses its tract value from the distribution $p_1(v) = 1$ on the interval $[0,1]$, and the other from $p_2(v) = 1/2$ on $[-\frac{1}{2}, \frac{3}{2}]$. Note that $v^* = 1/2$ for each bidder. The reaction functions for this example are graphed in Figure 3-4. The solution, by numerical approximation is $k_1 = .046$ and $k_2 = .727$. As can be seen, the bidder with the better information can place a bid closer to its estimate of tract value than the bidder with inferior information. It is also worth noting that when both bidders bid full value ($k_1 = k_2 = 0$), the first bidder's expected winning bid is $7/12$, while the second bidder expects to pay $23/24$. Thus, the second bidder should expect to make a larger correction in order to reach equilibrium, than the first bidder.

The other investigation of bidding with asymmetric information used a computer simulation. For this simulation, tract evaluations were generated according to equation 3:

$$(3) \qquad\qquad v_i = v^* + u_i.$$

The distribution of u_i was normal, with mean zero, but different bidders were assigned different variances, to simulate differences in information. Bids were calculated in accordance with equation 13:

$$(13) \qquad\qquad b_i = v_i - k_i.$$

Initially, all k_i were set equal to zero. After each simulated "auction" of 500 tracts, bidders compare their average winning bid to the hypothetical true value, v^*. Recall the assumption that bidders are able to learn v^* after they have won a tract. If a

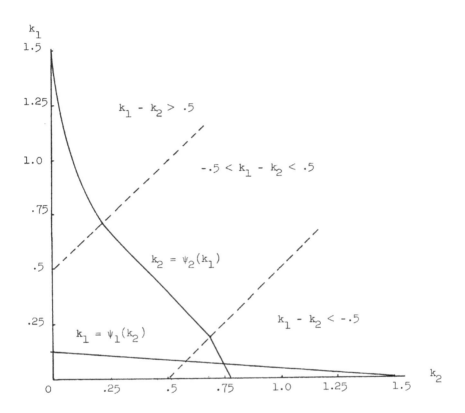

Figure 3-4. Bidding Reaction Functions:

Asymmetric Case. $N = 2$, $p_1(v) = 1$ on $[0,1]$,

$p_2(v) = \frac{1}{2}$ on $[-\frac{1}{2}, \frac{3}{2}]$.

Definitions for ψ_1 and ψ_2 on following page.

Figure 3-4 (continued)

ψ_1 is defined as follows:

$$k_1 = \tfrac{1}{2}[(1 + k_2) - \sqrt{(1 + k_2)^2 - \tfrac{1}{3}}],$$

for $-.5 < k_1 - k_2 < .5$;

$$k_1 = \frac{\tfrac{1}{2} - \tfrac{x^3}{6}}{1 - \tfrac{x^2}{2}} - \tfrac{1}{2}, \quad \text{for } k_1 - k_2 < -.5,$$

where $x = 1 + k_1 - k_2$.

ψ_2 is defined as follows:

$$k_2 = \frac{\tfrac{7}{3} - \tfrac{y}{4} - \tfrac{(1 - y)^3}{3}}{\tfrac{7}{4} + 3y - y^2} - \tfrac{1}{2}, \quad \text{for } k_1 - k_2 > .5$$

where $y = k_1 - k_2$;

$$k_2 = 1 - \sqrt{\tfrac{1}{12} + k_1^2}, \quad \text{for } -.5 < k_1 - k_2 < .5;$$

$$k_2 = \tfrac{3}{4} - \tfrac{k_1}{2}, \quad \text{for } k_1 - k_2 < -.5.$$

bidder discovers that he has been over bidding, he increases his adjustment factor, k_i, so that in future sales, there will be a greater difference between his estimate of tract value, and his bid. If the estimate of tract value is drawn from a normal distribution, then so is the bid for that tract. The adjustment factor k_i is a tool for shifting the mean of the distribution of bids (and hence also of winning bids) to the left. Figure 3-3 clearly shows this shift. Since following each simulated sale, all bidders choose new values for k_i, several iterations are required before an equilibrium is reached.

Table 3-2 summarizes the results of the simulation for five bidders, when two of the bidders have superior information. Two of the bidders select their estimated tract value from a distribution with a variance of .5, and the other three bidders have a variance of 1. All distributions are normal with mean ($v*$) equal to zero. Initially, with $k_1 = \cdots = k_5 = 0$, the bidders with less precise information concerning tract value won more often, but also paid too high a price. The bidders with smaller variance (better information) were clustered near the middle of all bids, as would be anticipated since all bidders are bidding their estimated tract value.

The overbidding problem explains the initial success of bidders with relatively poor information. Initially, bidders drawing estimates of tract value (and hence, bids) from distributions with large variances, draw some estimates which are extremely high.

Rank	Averages for Bidders with Variance = .5 (2 Bidders)		Averages for Bidders with Variance = 1. (3 Bidders)		Averages for All Bidders (5 Bidders)	
	Frequency	Bid	Frequency	Bid	Frequency	Bid
Initial Sale:						
1 (win)	.16	.86	.23	1.18	.20	1.08
2	.21	.24	.19	.48	.20	.46
3	.25	.02	.17	.05	.20	.03
4	.22	-.39	.19	- .47	.20	- .43
5	.16	-.82	.22	-1.13	.20	-1.03
Adjustment factor (k_i):	.00		.00			
Equilibrium:						
1 (win)	.33	- .02[a]	.11	.04[a]	.20	.00
2	.30	- .62	.14	- .59	.20	- .61
3	.21	-1.00	.19	-1.21	.20	-1.12
4	.11	-1.26	.26	-1.73	.20	-1.63
5	.05	-1.68	.30	-2.38	.20	-2.32
Adjustment factor (k_i):	-.621		1.485			

Table 3-2. Simulations of Auctions with Asymmetric Information
5 bidders: 2 bidders have variance = .5
3 bidders have variance = 1
$v^* = 0$ for all bidders.

[a] Average winning bid differs from $v^* = 0$ in equilibrium due to random error.

These high bids are easy winners, although they are destined to be unprofitable to the bidder, since they are so far above true tract value. By the same token, firms drawing bids from distributions with smaller variance are relatively unsuccessful at the start, since they do not draw such unusually high values.

After six simulated sales, the bidders had settled into an equilibrium in which all expected to pay $v^* = 0$ when they won. In this equilibrium, the better informed bidders won more often, and had higher bids when not winning than other bidders. The success of well informed bidders in equilibrium again results from the over-bidding problem. In the simulation reported in Table 3-2, the well informed bidders (variance = .5) subtracted an average of only .621 from their estimates of tract value, compared to 1.485 for the less accurate bidders. These corrections were sufficient to correct the overbidding problem for both types of bidders although those with poor information were unable to win a very large share of the tracts, and found that most of their bids ranked fourth or fifth.

In summary, the variance of a bidder's estimate of tract value reflects the accuracy of that estimate, which in turn depends on the amount of information available to the bidder. The more, and the better information used by a bidder in estimating tract value, the more accurate the estimate. The confidence which a bidder places in an estimate of tract value depends on the accuracy of that estimate. Bidders which make more accurate estimates will express their confidence by placing bids more nearly equal to those estimates than bidders less skillful in evaluating tracts.

4. A Bidding Model with Joint Ventures

As the reader may have surmised, joint ventures will be treated as bidders possessing more and better information to use in
tract evaluation than other bidders. The theory of the previous
section needs only to be reinterpreted to apply to sales in which
joint ventures participate. This section will distinguish two major
types of joint ventures, and will discuss the ways in which joint
ventures may use their superior information.

In Chapter II, four types of joint ventures formed for
bidding purposes were identified: Exploration and bidding joint
ventures, pure bidding joint ventures, investment joint ventures,
and joint ventures to guarantee supply of a product. The first two
of these types are by far the most important, and in fact, all
joint ventures could be classified as one of those two types. As
was discussed in Chapter II, exploration and bidding partnerships
(referred to hereafter as simply exploration joint ventures)
generally consist of firms which do not have the resources, either
financial or technical, to evaluate and bid on tracts singlehandedly.
These partnerships form more of necessity than convenience. Pure
bidding combines, on the other hand, consist of members which have
each completed their own tract analysis. These members may themselves be exploration joint ventures, which have decided not to
bid on their own, or they may be larger single firms, willing and
able to do their own exploration, but which again desire the security
of bidding in a group.

An important behavioral distinction is drawn between these two types of joint ventures. Exploration groups not joining with other partners for bidding, enter a sale with the same information as a single firm. All of the exploration, interpretation of maps, tract evaluation and bid preparation is done as a single unit, just as it would be by a single firm.

The pure bidding combine differs in one important respect from all other types of bidders. Members of a pure bidding joint venture have each done independent exploration on their own, prior to the formation of the bidding group. The joint venture uses these independent sets of data to finally evaluate each tract, and make a bid. Since a pure bidding joint venture calls on several independent sources of information, it can make more accurate estimates. As seen in the preceding section, the greater accuracy of value estimates relieves the bidding unit from some of its worry about overbidding, and means that its bid will be closer to its estimate of tract value.

The reader may ask why all bidders do not obtain several independent estimates of tract value, if improved information results in more winning bids and a higher probability of winning. The theory would certainly suggest this as a rational approach to the bidding problem. In practice, however, a single firm, or even a group of firms doing joint exploration, cannot make more than one truly independent estimate of a tract's value. When a single firm tries to reevaluate a tract, at some stage the same basic data, or the same personnel will come into play. Thus, attempts to make more

than one independent estimate of tract value will be biased by
the first estimate.

Pure bidding joint ventures are distinguished from all other
bidders, including both single firm bidders, and other joint ventures,
in that they alone are capable of gathering several independent
estimates of a tract's value. Pure bidding joint ventures should
be incorporated into the model of bidding with asymmetric information
in some way which reflects their improved information. Two possibilities will be discussed. First, a pure bidding joint venture may
average the estimates of value of its member firms, and second, the
joint venture may select the largest value estimate of the member
firms. In either case, the variance of the estimate is reduced.
The first procedure is unbiased, but the second introduces a bias.

Turning first to the straight averaging method, suppose a
pure bidding joint venture consists of n identical firms. Each
member draws its estimate of the logarithm of tract value from a
normal distribution $p(v)$, with mean v^*, and variance σ^2. Then the
joint venture's estimate of tract value, equal to the average of n
independent drawings from $p(v)$, would be distributed normally
with mean v^* and variance σ^2/n. The variance of the joint venture
is only $1/n$ times that of any member. If other bidders in the
sale draw their estimates of tract value from the same distribution
as members of the joint venture, then the joint venture's estimate
of value also has a variance which is $1/n$ times that of the other
bidders. The bidding joint venture has a much better ability to
predict tract value than other bidders, and correspond to a bidder

in the previous section with more accurate information.

The simulation reported in Table 3-2 can be interpreted as a sale in which two of the five bidders were joint ventures, consisting of two members each. Each joint venture estimated a tract's value by averaging two drawings from a standard normal probability distribution. Hence, the variances of the joint venture's value estimates equaled 1/2, compared to 1 for the other bidders. Table 3-3 presents an additional example. The setting is the same as table 3-2, except that the two joint ventures now each contain three members. Thus, the variance of each venture's estimate of tract value is reduced by a factor of 1/3. The effects of the improved information are even more pronounced in Table 3-3 than they were in Table 3-2. Once again, the joint ventures initially fare badly in the number of tracts they win, but do not overbid by as much as the other firms. In equilibrium, however, the joint ventures' average adjustment factor k_i is only about one-quarter that required by the other bidders. In equilibrium, when all bidders have adopted strategies which eliminate the overbidding problem, those bidders with better information (the joint ventures) win far more often than the other bidders. Each joint venture won an average of 38.5 percent of the tracts, compared to an average of 7.7 percent for the other bidders. On the other hand, since bidders with poorer information made a larger correction for overbidding, they frequently placed last or next to last, with very low bids.

Rather than straight averaging, a partnership might combine the independent tract evaluations provided by its members by

	Averages for Bidders with Variance = .33 (2 Bidders) (Joint Ventures)		Averages for Bidders with Variance = 1. (3 Bidders)		Averages for All Bidders (5 Bidders)	
	Frequency	Bid	Frequency	Bid	Frequency	Bid
Initial Sale:						
Rank: 1 (win)	.14	.67	.24	1.18	.20	1.03
2	.22	.34	.19	.49	.20	.43
3	.27	.02	.15	.03	.20	.03
4	.23	- .31	.18	- .46	.20	- .39
5	.14	- .66	.24	-1.12	.20	- .99
Adjustment factor (k_i):	.00		.00			
Equilibrium:						
Rank: 1 (win)	.38	- .02	.08	.04	.20	.00
2	.37	.56	.09	- .52	.20	- .55
3	.18	- .83	.21	-1.31	.20	-1.14
4	.06	-1.19	.29	-1.82	.20	-1.74
5	.01	-1.40	.33	-2.51	.20	-2.49
Adjustment factor (k_i):	.441		1.692			

Table 3-3. Simulations of Auctions with Joint Ventures (1):
5 bidders: 2 bidders (joint ventures) have variance = .33
3 bidders have variance = 1
$v^* = 0$ for all bidders.

choosing only the highest value. Several industry representatives with whom I discussed joint venture bidding stressed the fact that no firm was ever forced to bid less than it wanted to. Rather, some members of a joint venture, if they did not agree with a high bid for a particular tract, would drop out of the bidding for that tract, and let the rest of the joint venture go ahead with the bid. This behavior suggests that a joint venture would submit bids reflecting the highest estimate of each tract's value submitted by members.

Assume again that a joint venture consists of n identical members, each of which draws an estimate of tract value from the same probability distribution, $p(v)$. If the joint venture's estimate of tract value is simply the largest estimate drawn by the member, then the estimate made by the joint venture is distributed as the first order statistic of a sample of size n drawn from $p(v)$. As seen from Table 3-1, the first order statistic has a larger mean, but a smaller variance than the distribution $p(v)$. Note that the estimate of tract value made by the partnership is no longer unbiased, since the mean of $p(v)$ is v*, but the mean of the first order statistic is greater than v*.

Table 3-4 reports the results of a simulated auction in which two of the bidders were joint ventures consisting of three members each. Each joint venture estimated tract value by selecting the largest estimate of value made by its member firms. Since the member firms drew estimates from a standard normal distribution, the joint ventures' distributions of tract were approximately normal, with mean .85 and variance .56.[26] Since the joint ventures initially made

	Averages for Bidders with Variance = .56* (2 Bidders) (Joint Ventures)		Averages for Bidders with Variance = 1. (3 Bidders)		Averages for All Bidders (5 Bidders)	
	Frequency	Bid	Frequency	Bid	Frequency	Bid
Initial Sale:						
Rank: 1 (win)	.45	2.26	.04	1.98	.20	2.23
2	.38	1.52	.08	1.39	.20	1.49
3	.14	1.00	.24	.55	.20	.68
4	.03	.46	.32	- .08	.20	- .05
5	.00*	- .18	.33	- .83	.20	- .82
Adjustment factor (k_i):	.00		.00			
Equilibrium:						
Rank: 1 (win)	.38	- .03	.08	- .01	.20	- .03
2	.31	- .56	.12	- .70	.20	- .61
3	.18	-1.05	.21	-1.26	.20	-1.18
4	.10	-1.50	.27	-1.86	.20	-1.79
5	.03	-1.80	.32	-2.58	.20	-2.54
Adjustment factor (k_i):	1.404		1.665			

Table 3-4. Simulation of Auctions with Joint Ventures (2):
5 Bidders: 2 bidders (Joint Ventures) have variance = .56, mean = .85
2 bidders have variance = 1, mean = 0.
v* = 0 for all bidders.

biased estimates of tract value, it is not surprising that they
initially won a very large proportion of the tracts, and overbid
substantially. In the equilibrium, however, the smaller variance
of the joint ventures' estimates paid off. All bidders again paid
approximately v* for tracts which they won, but the joint ventures
won more frequently. The correction factors k_i for the joint
ventures are large enough to eliminate their overbidding problem,
even though the bias in their evaluation process compounds this
problem. Even in this case of a biased tract evaluation technique,
the job of the adjustment factor k_i is to shift the distribution of
bids to the left enough that the expected winning bid is just v*.
(See Figure 3-3 again).

In reality, pure bidding joint ventures use neither the straight
averaging nor the maximum value technique for estimating tract value.
Rather, what may be called a modified averaging takes place.
Certainly a joint venture will use all available information in
making the decision of what to bid, and will consider the independent
estimates submitted by each member. Each partner will produce its
own data, and indicate how its estimates were derived. Some errors
or faulty interpretations may be found, and there may be differences
of opinion in the individual estimates. In the final analysis, the
value estimated by the group will probably fall between the high
and low estimates of members. No theory can predict exactly where
in that range the joint venture's estimate will fall, but industry
representatives indicated to me that the estimates tend toward the
high side. The back-out back-in clauses in joint venture contracts

allow firms to drop out of a bid if they think it is too high. By
the same token, if a firm thinks the partnership is bidding too low,
it is welcome to submit a higher bid on its own. But this does not
mean that the highest value estimate will always be followed. If
one firm estimates a tract to be worth $50 million, and it joins
a partnership in which no other member estimates that tract's worth
at more than $30 million, that firm may be willing to revise its
estimate downward.

In conclusion, pure bidding joint ventures are unique among
bidders for offshore oil, in that they have access to several
independent estimates of each tract's value. Although no model can
completely capture the bidding process of these joint ventures, this
section has argued that their estimates of tract value are better,
in the sense of having smaller variance, than the estimates of other
bidders. Furthermore, the simulation model of an auction with asymmetric information suggests that bidders with better information are
able to win a larger share of the tracts, since such bidders have a
smaller risk of overbidding.

5. Summary of Testable Hypotheses

The theory of joint venture bidding developed in this chapter
suggests that bidders adopt a strategy which enables them to win
tracts without paying more than those tracts are worth. In order to
avoid overbidding, bidders learn over time that they should bid
only some fraction of their estimated tract value. The fraction of
estimated value which should be bid depends on the accuracy of the
estimate of value.

Pure bidding joint ventures, because of their position of having independent estimates of tract value, make more accurate estimates than other bidders, and bid a larger fraction of those estimates. Consequently, even though all bidders expect to pay the same amount for tracts which they win, pure bidding joint ventures expect to win a larger proportion of tracts than other bidders. Even when they do not win, these joint ventures expect to have relatively high bids, since they make only small corrections for overbidding. The following hypotheses will be tested in Chapter IV:

(1) Pure bidding joint ventures win with a greater share of their bids than other bidders, but

(2) Average winning bids of pure bidding joint ventures are the same as average winning bids of other bidders.

(3) Average non-winning bids of pure bidding joint ventures are larger than non-winning bids of other bidders.

One hypothesis which will not be tested is that bidders undergo a learning process, overbidding in early sales then revising their bids downward over time. Several problems prevent testing this hypothesis. First, to test the amount of overbidding requires that true tract value be known. True tract value is never known prior to a sale, and can only be calculated after all costs and revenues associated with a tract have become known, a process which could take many years.[27] The other problem with tracing the patterns of overbidding is that if the entire industry consistantly overbids, the result could be an increase in the price of the product rather than a reduction in future bids.

FOOTNOTES

1. For a bibliography of over 100 sources dealing with competitive bidding, see Robert M. Stark, "Competitive Bidding: A Comprehensive Bibliography," Operations Research, Vol. 19 (March-April, 1971), pp. 484-490. A good background may also be found in the section "A History of Sealed Bidding Models" of Thomas W. Ewart, Bidding for Oil Leases: A Simulation Approach, unpublished Ph.D. dissertation, Purdue University, 1972, pp. 12-24.

2. Charles Christenson, Strategic Aspects of Competitive Bidding for Corporate Securities. (Boston: Graduate School of Business Administration, Harvard University, 1965), p. 38.

3. J. H. Griesmer, R. E. Levitan and M. Shubik, "Toward a Study of Bidding Processes, Part IV: Game with Unknown Costs," Naval Research Logistics Quarterly, Vol. 14 (1967), p. 415.

4. Ibid., pp. 415-432. See also Griesmer and Shubik, "Toward A Study of Bidding Processes, Parts I-III," Naval Research Logistics Quarterly, Vol. 10 (1963), pp. 11-21, 151-173, 199-217.

5. W. Vickery, "Counterspeculation, Auctions, and Competitive Sealed Tenders," Journal of Finance, Vol. 16, No. 1 (March, 1971), pp. 8-37.

6. Robert B. Wilson, "Competitive Bidding with Asymmetric Information," Management Science, Vol. 13, No. 11 (July, 1967), pp. 816-820.

7. This type of asymmetry is also treated in Appendix III to Vickery, op. cit., p. 33.

8. See Chapter II, section 2 for a brief discussion of the value of so-called offset information. For an institutional account of bidding with asymmetric information, see D. H. Woods, Decision Making under Uncertainty in Heirarchical Organizations, dissertation, Harvard Business School, Boston, 1965, cited by R. B. Wilson, op. cit., p. 816.

9. Wilson, loc. cit.

10. Keith C. Brown, Bidding for Offshore Oil: Toward an Optimal Strategy. (Dallas: Southern Methodist University Press, 1969).

11. Ibid., p. 1.

12. F. Hanssmann and B. H. P. Rivett, "Competitive Bidding,"
    Operations Research Quarterly, Vol. 10 (March, 1959),
    pp. 49-55.

13. L. Friedman, _Competitive Bidding Strategies_, Ph.D. dissertation,
    Case Institute of Technology, 1957. Also see L. Friedman, "A
    Competitive Bidding Strategy," Journal of the Operations
    Research Society of America, Vol. 4, No. 1 (February, 1956),
    pp. 104-112.

14. Keith C. Brown, _op. cit._, p. 58.

15. John J. Arps, "A Strategy for Sealed Bidding," _Journal of
    Petroleum Technology_, (September, 1965), pp. 1033-1039.

16. In my interviews with industry representatives, I learned
    that exploration managers, whose job it is to find more oil
    reserves, may ask management to accept a _lower_ target profit
    rate, so that a higher bid would be justified for a particular
    offshore tract.

17. Keith C. Brown, "On Competitive Bidding Theory." Unpublished
    M. S., Purdue University, 1973, p. 3. Brown's paper deals
    with low-bid-win auctions, and I have taken the liberty of applying
    this to an offshore leasing sale. The same idea is expressed
    by Brown again in "A Note on the Apparent Bias of Net Revenue
    Estimates for Capital Investment Projects," _Journal of
    Finance_, Vol. 29, No. 4 (September, 1974), pp. 1215, 1216.

18. E. C. Capen, R. V. Clapp and W. M. Campbell, Competitive
    Bidding in High Risk Situations," _Journal of Petroleum
    Technology_, Vol. 23, (June, 1971), pp. 641-653.

19. _Ibid._, p. 643.

20. See footnotes 17 and 18 above.

21. E. C. Capen, _et. al._, _op. cit._, p. 643.

22. Distributions of first (largest) order statistics were first
    compiled in L. H. C. Tippett, "On the Extreme Individuals and
    the Range of Samples Taken from a Normal Population,"
    Biometrika, Vol. 17 (1925), pp. 364-387. See also Maurice A.
    Kendall, _The Advanced Theory of Statistics_. (Philadelphia:
    L. B. Lippincott Co., 1943), Chapter 14, "Order Statistics,"
    pp. 325-346; and Frederick Mosteller and R. K. E. Rourke,
    Sturdy Statistics: Nonparametrics and Order Statistics. (Reading,
    Mass.: Addison-Wesley Publishing Company, 1973), Chapters 14, 15.

23. Mosteller and Rourke, _op. cit._, p. 253.

24. Kendall, op. cit., p. 325.

25. E. C. Capen, et.al., op. cit., p. 647.

26. Joint ventures' estimates were distributed as the first order statistic of a sample of three drawn from a standard normal distribution. The figures for mean and variance come from Mosteller and Rourke, op. cit., pp. 356, 360.

27. For the possibilities of evaluating a tract after a sale, see Chapter IV, section 2, and Chapter IV, footnote 4.

CHAPTER IV

AN EMPIRICAL STUDY OF OFFSHORE LEASING SALES

According to the theory of competitive bidding developed in Chapter III, bidders with superior ability to judge the value of tracts offered for sale tend to win more often, and to rank higher when not winning than other bidders. Furthermore, Chapter III suggested that one group of bidders, pure bidding joint ventures, were better at tract evaluation by virtue of their access to several independent sets of exploration data.

This chapter tests the theoretical conclusions of Chapter III, using the record of bids compiled by the United States Department of Interior, covering all federal offshore sales. Section one of this chapter describes the data set.

Section two considers the need to control for tract quality, or true tract value. In the theoretical discussion of bidding, true tract value was assumed to be equal for all tracts. Tracts in an offshore sale do not, however, have the same true value. In order to compare bids across tracts, differences in bids resulting from different true values must be eliminated or controlled for.

Section three identifies several types of joint ventures which have bid in offshore sales. The characteristics of joint ventures which would classify them as pure bidding joint ventures are also examined.

Section four contains the major empirical tests of the theory in Chapter III. The major conclusions are that pure bidding joint ventures do in fact win more often and in general rank higher than their rivals, but the joint ventures' success comes at the expense of paying on average more for tracts won than other bidders. The latter result is at odds with the theory of Chapter III, in which all bidders expect to pay the same amount for tracts won.

Finally, the chapter concludes with a discussion of the costs and benefits of the prohibition of various types of joint ventures, including the recently proposed ban on joint ventures involving two or more major oil companies. Such a rule has been proposed by the Department of Interior, and is tentatively scheduled to take effect in the summer of 1975.[1]

1. The Department of Interior Data

Data employed in this chapter are published by the United States Department of Interior, in the Outer Continental Shelf Statistical Summary: 1954-1972, along with supplements issued following each federal offshore sale since 1972.[2] The book lists every bid placed in a federal offshore sale, along with the identity of the bidder. In the case of joint ventures, the several participants are all identified, along with their respective shares in the joint venture.

The sales included in the analysis are the thirteen major wildcat sales held between October, 1954 and December, 1973. Wildcat sales are those sales which offer tracts in relatively unexplored

areas. During this period, the government also held eleven so-
called drainage sales, in which tracts adjacent to previously
leased lands were sold. Drainage sales were excluded from the
current analysis, due to the asymmetric information, and the
peculiar bidding strategies adopted by many firms in drainage
sales. For a brief statistical description of all federal sales,
see table 2-1.

For the sales included in the analysis, the data set included
the following variables:[3]

(1) tract identification number;

(2) tract acreage;

(3) total bid (in dollars);

(4) rank of this bid among bids on the tract;

(5) total number of bids on the tract;

(6) oil company identification number;

(7) percentage interest of this firm in the bid;

(6') (7') if the bid was submitted by a joint venture, the
last two items are repeated until all members are included;

(8) dummy variable indicating whether the bid was
accepted or rejected by the government;

(9) sale date.

One variable frequently employed was the natural logarithm
of bid. Since bids are generally acknowledged to fit a lognormal
distribution, ℓn (bid) is approximately normal. Use of ℓn (bid)
rather than absolute bid eliminates the overwhelming influence of
large outliers in the data characteristic of a lognormally
distributed variable.

In some of the empirical work which follows, each bid was considered an observation, while at other times, observations were made on the basis of tracts. In addition, much of the analysis was done on a sale by sale basis, to avoid the uncontrollable effects of time on bidding behavior. Fortunately the quantity of data available permits this kind of breakdown. The data set for the thirteen sales consists of a total of 6756 wildcat bids on 1689 different tracts.

The data set was restricted for most calculations in two ways. First, all bids rejected by the government were eliminated. These bids do not reflect the "fair market value" of the tract offered according to the Department of Interior. Second, a large number of unrealistically small bids, placed by private individuals such as Fats Domino and Howell Spear, were eliminated. These bids, often as low as one dollar per acre, never won a tract, for even when they were the only bids on a tract, they were rejected. Any bid of less than $22,026 was arbitrarily classified as unrealistic, and was eliminated from the data set ($\ln(22026) = 10.0$). Table 4-1 indicates the numbers of observations eliminated from each sale. Unless otherwise specified, calculations use the net data set, after eliminating unrealistic and rejected bids.

2. Controlling for Tract Quality

In order to explain the amounts bid in offshore sales, and to measure the impact of joint ventures, tract quality is an essential variable. An estimate of tract quality probably influences a bid more than any other single factor.

Sale No.	Sale Date	Gross No. of Observations	No. of Wildcat Bonus Bids[a]	No. of Rejected &/or Unrealistic Bids[b]	Net No. of Observations
1	10/13/54	327	327	0	327
2	7/12/55	384	384	2	382
3	2/24/60	444	444	30	414
4	3/13/62	538	538	5	533
5	3/16/62	666	666	5	661
6	6/13/67	742	742	15	727
7	2/ 6/68	164	164	4	160
8	5/21/68	556	556	34	522
9	12/15/70	1043	1043	115	928
10	9/12/72	324	324	65	259
11	12/19/72	690	690	6	684
12	6/19/73	551	539	4	535
13	12/20/73	373	339	2	337
All Sales:		6802	6756	287	6469

Table 4-1: Adjustment of Data Set.

[a]Five and 12 drainage tracts, respectively, were offered in the 6/13/73 and 12/20/73 sales. These tracts are excluded from the analysis.

[b]Some bids were both unrealistic and rejected.

Neither of the two possible ways to directly estimate the quality, or true value of a tract proves to be practical. First, pre-sale data might be used to estimate tract value, much in the fashion that bidders themselves make their estimates. The detailed geological and financial data required for each tract to make such estimates are, however, unavailable, not to mention the great technical knowledge needed to analyze these data to make an estimate of tract value.

Alternatively, data available after a tract has been developed might be used to estimate how much the tract should have been worth at the time of its sale. Actual production and cost records of tracts leased are available, and could be used to calculate a present discounted value of a tract at its leasing date.[4] The major drawback to this method of estimating tract quality lies in the paucity of the data. As production from offshore tracts may continue for many years, only a relatively few tracts leased in federal offshore sales have completed their productive lives. Of course many tracts have been abandoned as being unproductive, but many other tracts leased as long ago as the 1950's remain in production. This makes a complete tabulation of discounted present value possible in only a few cases.

Having ruled out direct measurement, tract quality must be estimated by observing bidding behavior. More valuable tracts should be characterized by first, higher bids, and second more bids. First, since bids are based in part on a bidder's estimate of tract value, bids on a tract provide clues to the tract's worth.

Second, many bidders cannot afford to bid on all tracts in an auction,

and they must choose which tracts to bid on, and which to pass over.

Valuable tracts are likely to attract more bids than less valuable

ones.

The relationship between number of bidders and tract value

was first studied by Lawrence Friedman,[5] and later by Hanssmann and

Rivett.[6] These authors needed to predict the number of bidders on

a tract, based on the estimated value of the tract. Specifically,

Hanssmann and Rivett suggested that a bidder trying to estimate

the number of competitors it will face on a tract should:

(1) Determine established value (v).

(2) Use this estimated value to derive the expected
average bid (a).

(3) Use a ... to estimate the number of bidders (N).[7]

The present study proposes to reverse the procedure. In the

offshore sale data, the number of bidders, and amounts bid for

each tract are given. These data can be used to indicate the

value of a tract. Number of bidders and amount bid are,

however, highly correlated. Table 4-2 reports simple correlations

between number of bidders and two measures of amount bid: individual

bid, and winning bid per tract.

According to Chapter III, bidders hope to bid so that they

pay no more than the true tract value when they win. If this

behavior actually occurs, winning bid should be the most accurate

indication of tract value. Note that the correlation between number

Sale Date	Correlation of Number of Realistic Bids per Tract with:	
	Bid[a]	Winning Bid[b]
10/13/54	.40	.78
7/12/55	.45	.77
2/24/60	.39	.69
3/13/62	.20	.49
3/16/62	.41	.72
6/13/67	.33	.60
2/ 6/68	.50	.76
5/21/68	.41	.77
12/15/70	.31	.61
9/12/72	.34	.71
12/19/72	.41	.70
6/19/73	.50	.82
12/20/73	.30	.54
	—	—
All Sales	.33	.52

Table 4-2: Correlation between Number of Bidders and
Amount Bid.[c]

[a]Calculated using each bid in the sale.
[b]Calculated using each tract in the sale.
[c]Includes net data set. See Table 4-1.

of bidders and winning bid is consistantly higher than the correlation
with all bids.

To summarize, Table 4-2 shows the relationship between number
of bidders and amount bid. Also, there is an obvious relationship
between amount bid and tract value. As Hanssmann and Rivett have
shown, a positive relationship exists between number of bidders and
tract value. For these reasons, number of bidders will be used
in subsequent analysis as a controlling variable for tract value.
It is important to stress that no causality is implied. Increased
numbers of bidders do not cause a tract to become more valuable.
Were any causality to be discussed, it would probably run from
value to number of bidders. The lack of causality does not, however,
lesses the ability of number of bidders to control for tract
value.

As a final remark on controlling for tract value, no attempt
will be made to assess the extent to which a tract might be truly
more valuable to one bidder than another. The true value of a
tract is assumed to be the same for all bidders. True value depends
on the actual amount of recoverable reserves available, the actual
cost of extraction, the actual timing of exploration, development
and production, all of which become known only after the auction,
but which are assumed to be independent of the winning bidder.

3. The Types of Joint Ventures

Recall the two major types of joint ventures discussed in Chapter III: the pure bidding joint venture, characterized by its several independent sets of data; and the exploration and bidding partnership. The latter behaved in the same manner as a single firm, while the former, by pooling its sets of information, proved superior in evaluating tracts. Results of simulated sales showed that pure bidding joint ventures had more success in winning tracts, and ranked higher on average than other bidders.

The data show that many different joint ventures have been formed for bidding in offshore sales. Some way must be found to classify each of these partnerships into one of the two major types. Single firms are easily distinguished from joint ventures, but to separate pure bidding from exploration and bidding joint ventures requires an assumption based on the bidding behavior reported by the oil companies themselves. Generalizing from my interviews with participants in offshore sales, independent oil companies tend to form exploration and bidding joint ventures, while major oil companies prefer to carry out their own exploration and enter joint ventures purely for the purpose of bidding on (and later developing) tracts. Occasionally a joint venture may exhibit a mixture of the two types of behavior in which some members of a pure bidding joint venture are themselves joint ventures which have carried out exploration. This mixture does not change the fact that the partnership draws on several independent sources of information, but the number of member firms does not always accurately reflect the number of independent sets of exploration data available. This study will identify pure bidding joint ventures as those joint ventures which contain at least one major oil company.

Of course identifying pure bidding joint ventures as those containing major oil companies is not completely accurate. Some major oil companies do form partnerships for the purpose of exploration as well as for bidding. Less frequently, independent firms may undertake their own exploration and tract evaluation, subsequently joining a partnership for bidding. There is no way to judge the extent of these exceptions, but I believe it reasonable to assume that pure bidding joint ventures are those which contain major oil companies.

Specifying which oil companies to include under the heading "major" poses the next problem in the identification of pure bidding joint ventures. The distinction between "major" and "independent" oil companies is one of degree rather than one of kind. For this study, "major" was taken to be one of the largest seven oil companies, ranked by sales. Table 4-3 lists the 20 largest companies which bid frequently in offshore sales. The decision to call the top seven companies "major" was made for several reasons. First, the same seven oil companies have led the industry in dollar sales, as measured by Fortune magazine, since the first offshore auction in 1954, although the order within those seven has changed. The rankings have been not

Company	1974 Sales[a] ($ billion)	1973 Refining Capacity[b] (million bbl/day)	1973 No. of Refineries[b]	1973 Worldwide Production (million bbl/day)[c]
Exxon	42.1	1.25	5	6.37
Texaco	23.3	1.08	12	4.51
Mobil	18.9	.93	8	2.46
Stand. Calif.	17.2	.98	12	3.82
Gulf	16.5	.86	8	2.58
Stand. Ind.	9.1	1.06	10	.87
Shell	7.6	1.11	8	1.00
Continental	7.0	.35	7	.59
Arco	6.7	.79	6	.60
Occidental	5.7	.12[c]	na	.25
Tenneco	5.0	.08[c]	1[c]	.09
Phillips	5.0	.40	6	.36
Union	4.4	.49	4	.36
Sun	3.8	.48	5	.37
Amarada Hess	3.7	.80[c]	na	.15
Ashland	3.2	.36	7	.05
Marathon	2.9	.31	3	.44
Cities Service	2.8	.27	1	.22
Getty	2.7	.26[c]	na	.43
Stand. Ohio	2.2	.38	4	.05

Table 4-3: Companies Participating in Offshore Sales.

[a]Source: "The Fortune Directory of the 500 Largest Industrial Corporation," Fortune, May 1975, p. 208

[b]Source: Standard and Poor's Industry Surveys: Oil, Basic Analysis, July 4, 1974, p. 68.

[c]Source: Individual Corporate Reports, 1974.

[na]Not Available

nearly so consistent in the rest of the industry, in part due to a large number of mergers in the 1960's. A second, and more compelling reason for choosing this definition of "major" comes from the Department of Interior, which has accepted the same definition, based on proven hydrocarbon reserves.[8] Pure bidding joint ventures are, then, those partnerships which contain at least one of the seven major oil companies.

Table 4-4 lists some of the more frequent exploration and bidding joint ventures appearing in recent sales. Some of these partnerships have endured for many years, and most of them last for several sales. The firms in parentheses were only occasionally members of a particular joint venture, and some firms have been members of more than one of the groups. For the most part, however, joint ventures formed by independent oil companies, tend to be more stable and long lasting than those involving majors. In fact, majors frequently can be found in several different joint ventures in a single sale for bidding on different tracts. The relative instability of joint ventures involving the majors supports the contention that these partnerships do not perform any exploration, but form only for bidding purposes. Similarly, the longer lived partnerships among independents suggest that resources are being pooled not only for bidding, but also for exploration.

This section has suggested a method of distinguishing pure bidding from exploration and bidding joint ventures, by defining pure bidding joint ventures as those which contain one or more

General American
of Texas
Burmah Development

Allied Chemical
Clark Producing
Sonat Exploration
Tesoro

Kerr-McGee
Cabot Corporation
Felmont
Case Poneroy
Forest

Continental
Arco
Getty
Cities Service

Columbia Gas
Energy Ventures
Forest

Signal
Amarada Hess
Marathon
Texas Eastern
Texas Pacific
Louisiana Land and
  Exploration Co.
(El Paso Natural Gas)
(C.N.G. Producing)

Newmont
Midwest
Southland Royalty
Champlin
Offshore
Sonat
Samedian

General American
Aztec
Pelto
Consolidated Gas

Ashland
Burmah
Texas Prod.
Penzoil
Mesa

Quintana
Canadian Occidental
(Skelly)
(Sun)
(Cities Service)
(Getty)

Superior
Ashland
Hunt
Placid
Highland
General Crude
Canadian Superior
Hamilton Bros.
Kewanee
Trans Ocean
(General American)
(Cabot)
(L. V. O.)
(Bass Enterprise)
(Koch)
(Unidel)
(American Natural Gas)
(Trend)
(Getty)

Table 4-4. Frequent Joint Ventures among Independent Oil Companies. From the five major sales from 1970-1973.

(Firms in parentheses were occasional partners.)

of the seven major oil companies. Section 4 tests some hypotheses concerning the theoretical bidding behavior of pure bidding joint ventures developed in Chapter III.

4. The Relative Success of Pure Bidding Joint Ventures

This section compares the bidding behavior of joint ventures formed purely for bidding to that of all other bidders. Pure bidding joint ventures (PBJVs), as discussed in section 3, include one or more of the seven major oil companies. Non-PBJV bidders include joint ventures among independent oil companies, and all firms which bid alone.

The theoretical predictions of Chapter III state that bidders attempt to prevent overbidding. If firms bid exactly what they estimated a tract was worth, then winning bidders would consistently find that they had paid too much. To correct for the overbidding problem, firms bid less than their estimate of a tract value, with the amount of reduction depending on the accuracy of their original estimate. PBJVs, since they estimate tract value by averaging their members independent evaluations, have less fear of overbidding than other bidders.

Although all bidders expect to pay the same amount in winning a particular tract, the theory predicts that losing bids by PBJV's should be larger than losing bids by other bidders.

Using data from the thirteen major wildcat sales from 1954 to 1973, frequency distributions of bids can be constructed for each of the two types of bidders. Table 4-5 presents the overall distribution of all bids in those thirteen sales, broken down by type of bidder, and by rank of bid. Of course there are more first place bids than second, and so forth, since the table includes all tracts, regardless of numbers of bidders. The table also includes the average ℓn (bid) for each type of bidder and bid rank.

In comparing the frequency distributions of bids by PBJVs and others, note that PBJVs rank first, second and third relatively more frequently than the other bidders, as expected from the theory. PBJVs, with their superior information, place bids closer to pre-sale estimated values than others.

Surprising, however, is the extent to which winning bids by PBJVs exceed winning bids of other sale participants. Although winning bids were expected to be equal for all bidders, Table 4-5 shows that PBJVs pay substantially more for tracts which they win, especially in dollar terms. The antilog of 14.84 is approximately $2.8 million. This figure is the geometric mean winning bid of PBJVs. The corresponding figure for other bidders is the antilog of 13.92, or $1.1 million.

Several factors might explain the large difference in average winning bid between the two types of bidders. First, PBJVs might place higher true values on tracts. Recall that it was assumed that all bidders would value tracts equally if they had perfect information. If tracts are inherently more valuable for PBJVs, the difference in average winning bid could be accounted for. Alternatively, tracts which PBJVs win may be qualitatively different from those won by other bidders. If PBJVs choose to

Rank	Number of Bids in this Rank[a]	Averages for Pure Bidding Joint Ventures		Averages for All Other Bidders		Averages for All Bidders	
		Freq.	Bid[b]	Freq.	Bid[b]	Freq.	Bid[b]
1 (win)	1576	.28	14.84	.24	13.92	.24	14.10
2	1139	.22.	14.62	.17	13.74	.18	13.92
3	858	.14	14.56	.13	13.79	.13	13.93
4	694	.11	14.55	.11	13.73	.11	13.87
5	544	.08	14.37	.09	13.75	.08	13.84
6	420	.05	14.67	.07	13.79	.06	13.90
7	343	.03	14.28	.06	13.87	.05	13.92
8	264	.04	14.57	.04	13.82	.04	13.94
9	204	.02	15.30	.03	13.75	.03	13.92
10	156	.01	14.00	.03	13.93	.02	13.94
11	106	.01	15.13	.02	13.69	.02	13.88
12	75	(c)	14.61	.01	13.88	.01	13.92
13	48	(c)	15.12	.01	13.85	.01	13.98
14	24	(c)	14.97	(c)	13.48	(c)	13.79
15	11	.00	---	(c)	13.85	(c)	13.85
16	6	.00	---	(c)	12.11	(c)	12.11
17	1	.00	---	(c)	10.33	(c)	10.33
Total		1.00	14.65	1.00	13.81	1.00	13.95
No. of Bids	6469	1106		5363		6469	

Table 4-5: Frequency Distributions and Averages of All Bids, by Bidder Type and Bid Rank.

[a]Includes all accepted, realistic, bonus bids on wildcat tracts in thirteen major sales from 1954 - 1973. See Table 4-1.

[b]Figures reported are averages of natural logarithms.

[c]Less than .005.

bid on more valuable tracts, then they would be expected to pay more when they win. Finally, PBJVs might simply fail to correct for the overbidding problem, and pay more than the worth of the tracts.

The most obvious problem with Table 4-5 is that it covers a span of 20 years. A glance at Tables 2-1 and 2-3 shows that two trends have taken place over time. First, the amounts bid for offshore tracts has risen dramatically (Table 2-1). Second, the share of bids coming from joint ventures has also risen (Table 2-3). These two trends together imply that a relatively large share of the recent, expensive tracts have been purchased by joint ventures. Thus, trends over time may account for much of the difference between the levels of winning bids in Table 4-5.

The inclusion of unrealistic and rejected bids, since all of the 164 unrealistic bids, and all but seven of the 140 rejected bids were placed by non-PBJV bidders. Including these low bids pulls down the averages for the other bidders.

Table 4-6 corrects for the problem of time trend in Table 4-5 by dealing with only a limited number of years. Only the five major sales in the years from 1970 to 1973 are included in Table 4-6. During this period, both the amounts paid for offshore tracts, and the share of bids placed by joint ventures remained relatively stable. Consequently, any differences in amounts paid for tracts won should not be caused by trends over time.

Rank	No. of Bids in this Rank[a]	Averages for PBJVs		Averages for All Other Bidders		Averages for All Bidders	
		Freq.	Bid[b]	Freq.	Bid[b]	Freq.	Bid[b]
1 (win)	468	.23	15.83	.15	15.53	.17	15.62
2	393	.20	15.55	.13	15.10	.14	15.24
3	345	.14	15.07	.12	14.94	.13	14.97
4	297	.12	15.10	.11	14.80	.11	14.87
5	251	.09	15.05	.09	14.69	.09	14.77
6	210	.06	15.32	.08	14.60	.08	14.74
7	180	.04	14.82	.07	14.67	.07	14.69
8	149	.04	15.26	.06	14.50	.05	14.62
9	126	.03	15.52	.05	14.26	.05	14.46
10	102	.01	14.74	.04	14.44	.04	14.47
11	75	.02	15.31	.03	14.18	.03	14.38
12	61	.01	14.92	.03	14.14	.02	14.20
13	45	.01	15.12	.02	13.92	.02	14.05
14	23	.01	14.97	.01	13.53	.01	13.84
15	11	.00	---	.01	13.85	(c)	13.85
16	6	.00	---	(c)	12.11	(c)	12.11
17	1	.00	---	(c)	10.33	(c)	10.33
Total		1.00	15.37	1.00	14.79	1.00	14.92
No. of Bids 2743		625		2118		2743	

Table 4-6: Frequency Distributions and Averages of All Bids, by Bidder Type and Bid Rank, for Five Recent Sales.

[a]Includes all accepted, realistic, bonus bids on wildcat tracts in five major sales from 1970 to 1973.

[b]Figures reported are averages of natural logarithms.

[c]Less than .005.

In Table 4-6, PBJVs rank first through fourth more frequently than other bidders, while the other bidders are more frequently found in sixth place or lower. The Chi-square test shows that the two distributions of bids by rank would occur by chance less than one time in two hundred ($X^2_{16} = 87.5$).

The surprising gap between average winning bids found in Table 4-5 is less in Table 4-6, but not eliminated. PBJVs now average 15.83 ($7.5 million) in winning, while others average 15.53 ($5.6 million), still a large difference. The possibility remains that PBJVs bid on, and win, more valuable tracts, accounting for their higher average winning bids. Neither Table 4-5 nor Table 4-6 controls for tract quality, since both include all bids on all tracts. If indeed it can be shown that PBJVs do bid on more valuable tracts, then some control for tract quality should be introduced.

Section two of this Chapter discussed the use of number of bidders as an indication of tract quality, since valuable tracts would attract more bidders. Table 4-7 classifies the bids of each bidding type into three broad quality groups, based on the number of opponents faced. The figures show that PBJVs tend to place bids on lower quality tracts (i.e., face less competition). The argument that PBJVs bid on more valuable tracts, and therefore have higher average winning bids does not hold, since PBJVs do not appear to bid on more valuable tracts.

Although Table 4-7 does not clear up the problem of different expected winning bids across bidder types it does indicate that

Number of Bidders, N[a] (Proxy for Tract Quality)	Pure Bidding Joint Ventures	Other Bidders	All Bidders
$1 \leq N \leq 5$ (Low Quality)	33%	24%	26%
$6 \leq N \leq 10$ (Medium Quality)	39%	39%	39%
$11 \leq N$ (High Quality)	28%	38%	35%
	100%	100%	100%
Total Number of Bids (100%)	625	2118	2743

Table 4-7: Distribution of Bids by Tract Quality.[b]

[a]Number of opponents = N - 1.

[b]Using same data as Table 4-6.

non-PBJV bidders tend to bid on more valuable tracts, and that tract quality should be controlled. Table 4-8 selects only those tracts which received exactly five realistic bids, and reports frequency distributions and average bids. Holding number of bidders constant attempts to control for tract quality.

Table 4-8 shows once again that PBJVs win more often, and bid more and rank higher than other bidders when not winning. The difference between average winning bids persists. The Chi-square test for difference in the two frequency distributions shows that the observed frequencies could arise by chance about twenty-eight times in one hundred (X_4^2 = 5.03). Although the number five was selected arbitrarily, controlling on other numbers of bidders produces tables similar to Table 4-8 in most cases.

Another statistical procedure useful for investigating the bidding behavior of PBJVs is linear regression. Using regression analysis, the two hypotheses that losing bids by PBJVs are larger than losing bids of other bidders, and that average winning bids are the same for all types of bidders, will be tested. The first models tested relate to the level of non-winning bids. Model 1 uses non-winning bid (in thousands of dollars) as the dependent variable, while the dependent variable in model 2 is the natural logarithm of non-winning bid (in dollars). The independent variables are the same for both models, and include two measures of tract quality, and a dummy variable for whether the bid was placed by a PBJV. The measures of tract quality are the number of bidders on the tract, and the number of acres. Models 1 and 2 have

	Averages for Pure Bidding Joint Ventures		Averages for All Other Bidders		Averages for All Bidders	
	Freq.	Bid[a]	Freq.	Bid[a]	Freq.	Bid[a]
Rank: 1 (win)	.28	15.53	.17	15.35	.20	15.41
2	.24	14.99	.19	14.79	.20	14.85
3	.20	14.49	.20	14.39	.20	14.41
4	.14	13.74	.22	14.00	.20	13.95
5	.14	13.46	.22	13.00	.20	13.08
Total	1.00	14.66	1.00	14.24	1.00	14.34
Number of Bids	50		155		205	

Table 4-8: Frequency Distributions and Average Bids on Tracts Receiving Exactly Five Bids (Five recent sales).[b]

[a]Figures reported are averages of natural logarithms of bids.

[b]Sales included are from 1970 – 1973.

the following form:

(1) $B = \alpha_o + \alpha_1 N + \alpha_2 A + \alpha_3 D + u_\alpha;$

(2) $\ln(B) = \beta_o + \beta_1 N + \beta_2 A + \beta_3 D + u_\beta;$

where:

   B = non-winning bid (in \$ thousands);

   $\ln(B)$ = natural logarithm of non-winning bid (in dollars);

   N = number of realistic bids;

   A = acres;

   D = PBJV dummy (1 = PBJV);

u_α, u_β = disturbance terms.

The impact of PBJVs on the level of losing bids can be determined from the coefficients α_3 and β_3. In model 1, α_3 simply represents the average difference (in thousands of dollars) between PBJV bids and other bids. Model 2 can be rewritten:

$$B = e^{\beta_o} \cdot e^{\beta_1 N} \cdot e^{\beta_2 A} \cdot e^{\beta_3 D} \cdot e^{u_\beta}.$$

Thus, a PBJV effects the dollar bid by a multiplicative factor, e^{β_3}. A value of $\beta_3 < 0$ implies that PBJVs bid less than other bidders, $\beta_3 = 0$ implies no difference in bidding behavior and $\beta_3 > 0$ indicates that PBJVs bid more.

Variations in hydrocarbon prices, equipment costs, technology and uncertainty from sale to sale all effect the level of bids, both winning and losing, but are not included in models 1 or 2. Rather than deal with these variables, and since there was sufficient data, the models were estimated independently for each of the thirteen major sales.

The estimated coefficients for models 1 and 2 are presented in Tables 4-9 and 4-10 respectively. In both cases, the most significant variable in explaining losing bid level is number of bids. The coefficients of D, the PBJV dummy are positive in nearly all cases, but often lack significance. PBJVs appear to have a moderate positive effect on the level of losing bids.

Models 1 and 2 were run again on the entire data set for all 13 sales, introducing a trend variable, which was the last two digits of the year in which the sale was held. All coefficients in these models, reported in Table 4-11, were significant at the 1 percent level, and once more show the positive influence of PBJVs on losing bids.

The theory of joint venture bidding predicts that PBJVs should bid more, when not winning. This prediction is supported by Tables 4-9 to 4-11. On winning bids, however, adjustments for the overbidding problem should insure that all bidders pay the same amounts. Models 3 and 4 focus only on winning bids (WB), and the coefficients of the dummy variable for PBJVs should equal zero in these models:

$$(3) \qquad WB = \gamma_0 + \gamma_1 N + \gamma_2 A + \gamma_3 D + u_\gamma$$

$$(4) \qquad \ell n(WB) = \delta_0 + \delta_1 N + \delta_2 A + \delta_3 D + u_\delta$$

Tables 4-12 and 4-13 report the results of models 3 and 4. Number of bids is again the most influential independent variable.

Coefficient of Variable

Sale No.[a]	Const.	No. of Bids	Acres	PBJV Dummy	R^2	No. of Observations
1	-790	166** (22)	.094 (.059)	101 (377)	.20	237
2	-1593	234** (29)	.364* (.080)	-477** (186)	.24	261
3	-1040	337** (41)	.070 (.121)	342 (233)	.20	267
4	- 137	75** (16)	.026 (.091)	316** (149)	.07	327
5	-1086	228** (21)	.073 (.082)	860** (189)	.24	456
6	-1554	332** (39)	.191 (.185)	38 (407)	.11	569
7	-13271	3624** (915)	1.254 (1.213)	1369 (2427)	.15	89
8	-2296	524** (57)	.081 (.184)	1680** (631)	.21	412
9	-1437	352** (29)	.041 (.118)	631* (368)	.16	809
10	2331	674** (108)	-.622 (.571)	1916** (915)	.16	197
11	641	1393 (109)	-1.250 (.560)	3053** (837)	.22	568
12	-2368	1439** (110)	-.318 (.941)	1531 (1037)	.29	439
13	-11851	2307** (307)	No Variance	7318** (1353)	.21	262

Table 4-9: Estimated Coefficients of Model 1:[b]

$$B = \alpha_o + \alpha_1 N + \alpha_2 A + \alpha_3 D + u_\alpha$$

(Standard errors of estimate in parentheses)

[a]For sale dates, see Table 4-1   *Significant at 5 percent level.

[b]For definitions of variables, see text.   **Significant at 1 percent level.

Coefficient of Variable

Sale No.[a]	Const.	No. of Bids	Acres	PBJV Dummy	R^2
1	10.44	.22** (.03)	.00019** (.00008)	-.35 (.50)	.21
2	9.86	.33** (.03)	.00026** (.00009)	-.23 (.20)	.30
3	10.15	.30** (.03)	.00025** (.00009)	.40** (.17)	.30
4	10.46	.12** (.02)	.00025** (.00010)	.33* (.17)	.16
5	10.06	.26** (.02)	.00023** (.00006)	.63** (.15)	.39
6	11.57	.20** (.01)	.00010 (.00007)	.15 (.15)	.25
7	10.38	.78** (.13)	.00016 (.00017)	.71** (.34)	.32
8	10.89	.20** (.02)	.00025** (.00005)	.30* (.17)	.38
9	11.46	.16** (.01)	.00018** (.00005)	.63** (.15)	.20
10	13.85	.15** (.02)	-.00007 (.00010)	.50** (.17)	.23
11	13.62	.20** (.01)	-.00005 (.00007)	.19* (.10)	.30
12	13.85	.16** (.01)	.00003 (.00009)	.03 (.10)	.37
13	12.05	.34** (.04)	No Variance	.97** (.15)	.30

Table 4-10: Estimated Coefficients of Model 2:[b]

$$\ln(B) = \beta_o + \beta_1 N + \beta_2 A + \beta_3 D + u_\beta.$$

(Standard errors of estimate in parentheses.)

See notes and number of observations on Table 4-9

Coefficient of Variable:

Model	Dependent Variable	Const.	No. of Bids	Acres	PBJV Dummy	Year	R^2	No. of Observations
1'	B	-20395	444** (24)	.28** (.10)	2769** (249)	280** (18)	.19	4856
2'	$\ell n(B)$	4.68	.14** (.005)	.00013** (.00002)	.56** (.05)	.11** (.004)	.42	4856

Table 4-11: Estimated Coefficients of Models 1' and 2':[b]

(1') $B = \alpha_o + \alpha_1 N + \alpha_2 A + \alpha_3 D + \alpha_4 Y + u_\alpha$

(2') $\ell n(B) = \beta_o + \beta_1 N + \beta_2 A + \beta_3 D + \beta_4 Y + u_\beta$

(Standard errors of estimate in parentheses.)

See notes on Table 4-9.

Coefficients of Variable

Sale No.[a]	Const.	No. of Bids	Acres	PBJV Dummy	R^2	No. of Observations
1	-268	409** (39)	.012 (.093)	547 (506)	.60	90
2	-891	436** (32)	.138** (.058)	-459* (255)	.62	121
3	-1149	899** (79)	.120 (.157)	-196 (410)	.47	147
4	-292	373** (49)	.049 (.109)	-493 (371)	.24	206
5	-1617	600** (42)	.213 (.131)	11 (338)	.52	205
6	-2551	865** (93)	.404 (.408)	-1281 (1155)	.36	158
7	-4861	7914** (818)	-.180 (1.003)	-5498** (2301)	.59	71
8	-3349	1953** (183)	-.142 (.352)	1370 (1696)	.58	110
9	-2226	1057** (127)	.307 (.608)	-2067 (1489)	.36	119
10	-273	2961** (361)	-1.210 (1.519)	5059** (2486)	.52	62
11	-1759	2890** (286)	-.344 (1.422)	2263 (2477)	.48	116
12	3668	3422** (256)	.073 (1.393)	2299 (3833)	.67	96
13	-13349	6071** (1218)	No Variance	5299 (7021)	.28	75

Table 4-12: Estimated Coefficients of Model 3.

$$WB = \gamma_o + \gamma_1 N + \gamma_2 A + \gamma_3 D + u_\gamma.$$

(Standard errors of estimate in parentheses.)

[a] For sale dates see Table 4-1.

* Significant at 5 percent level.

** Significant at 1 percent level.

Coefficient of Variable

Sale No.[a]	Const.	No. of Bids	Acres	PBJV Dummy	R^2
1	12.44	.34** (.04)	-.00007 (.00009)	-.23 (.46)	.54
2	10.34	.49** (.03)	.00024** (.00005)	-.18 (.24)	.69
3	11.00	.48** (.04)	.00024** (.00009)	-.34 (.23)	.47
4	10.91	.30** (.03)	.00026** (.00007)	-.38 (.24)	.39
5	10.11	.39** (.02)	.00037** (.00008)	.61** (.19)	.62
6	12.19	.27** (.02)	.00016* (.00009)	-.30 (.25)	.54
7	12.66	1.01** (.09)	.00004 (.00011)	-.97** (.25)	.68
8	11.03	.34** (.02)	.00033** (.00004)	.43** (.18)	.86
9	12.38	.18** (.02)	.00033** (.00008)	-.35 (.21)	.51
10	14.26	.25** (.03)	-.00001 (.00012)	.26 (.20)	.55
11	14.69	.23** (.02)	-.00004 (.00009)	.21 (.16)	.59
12	13.44	.22** (.02)	.00022** (.00010)	.16 (.26)	.67
13	13.38	.42** (.04)	No Variance	.46** (.21)	.68

Table 4-13: Estimated Coefficients for Model 4.

$$\ln(WB) = \delta_o + \delta_1 N + \delta_2 A + \delta_3 D + u_\delta$$

(Standard errors of estimate in parenthesis)

For notes and number of observations, see Table 4-12.

The coefficients on the PBJV show no clear tendency to be either positive or negative. About half have positive signs, and half are negative, although of the six coefficients which are significant at the 5 percent level or better, four are positive. The hypothesis that γ_3 and δ_3 should be zero cannot be rejected with these models.

Two new models, 3' and 4', which included a time variable were estimated using data for all 1576 winning bids. These results are contained in Table 4-14. All coefficients in both of these models, including γ_3 and δ_3, are significantly greater than zero.

According to the estimates of the coefficients α_3 and γ_3 in models 1' and 3' (Tables 4-11 and 4-14), the absolute difference between bids of PBJVs and other bidders is about the same for winning bids ($\hat{\gamma}_3$ = \$2,828 million) and for losing bids ($\hat{\alpha}_3$ = \$2,976 million). In relative terms, however, models 2' and 4' show that the winning bids are closer together. For losing bids, PBJVs effect ℓnB by $\hat{\beta}_3$ = .61, or taking antilogarithms, they effect dollars bid by a factor of $e^{.61}$ = 1.84. That is, losing bids by PBJVs tend to be 84 percent higher than bids by other bidders. For winning bids, however, $\hat{\delta}_4$ = .25, and $e^{.25}$ = 1.28. Thus PBJVs' _winning_ bids tend to be only 28 percent higher than other winning bids.

The analysis of this section shows that bidders with better information (pure bidding joint ventures) do tend to win more often, and to place higher bids when not winning, all as expected. It also suggests that PBJVs pay more for tracts which they win than do other bidders, a fact not predicted by the theory, although evidence on this point is not conclusive.

Coefficient of Variable

Dependent Variable	Const.	No. of Bids	Acres	PBJV Dummy	Year	R^2	No. of Observations
Win Bid	-32275	1620** (77)	.482** (.236)	2828** (657)	435** (47)	.34	1576
ℓn(Win Bid)	4.94	.30** (.008)	.00022** (.00002)	.25** (.07)	.11** (.005)	.66	1576

Table 4-14: Estimated Coefficients of Models 3' and 4':

(3') $WB = \gamma_0 + \gamma_1 N + \gamma_2 A + \gamma_3 D + \gamma_4 Y + u_\gamma;$

(4') $\ell n(WB) = \delta_0 + \delta_1 N + \delta_2 A + \delta_3 D + \delta_4 Y + u_\delta;$

(Standard errors of estimate in parentheses.)

See notes on Table 4-12.

A possible explanation for the difference in winning bids across bidding types may lie in the treatment of risk by the different types. If pure bidding joint ventures are less risk averse, or more willing to assume risk, due to their broader base of support (major oil companies), they might be willing to pay more for a tract than some other bidders. This returns to the point made originally in connection with Table 4-5, that one factor contributing to the differences in winning bids might be that pure bidding joint ventures place higher true values on tracts.

5. A Note on Different Types of Bidders

The analysis so far has considered only two types of bidders: pure bidding joint ventures, and all other bidders. This distinction followed from the argument that: (1) bidders with superior information bid differently from other bidders; and (2) pure bidding joint ventures (those containing major oil companies) possessed superior information.

The data permit a further breakdown of bidding types. Two varieties of pure bidding joint ventures exist: joint ventures containing only major oil companies, called major joint ventures; and joint ventures consisting of both majors and independents, called mixed joint ventures. Also non-PBJVs can be divided into three sub-types: major oil companies bidding alone, independents bidding alone, and joint ventures consisting only of independents. Although this detailed a breakdown leaves some categories with few observations, some interesting conclusions can be drawn.

Tables 4-15a and 4-15b expand the information presented in Table 4-6. Note first, that although joint ventures including only major firms are rare (only 1.4 percent of all bids came from such partnerships), they are generally quite successful, winning on half of their bids. The success of the major joint ventures is measured not only by their frequent wins, but also by their ability to consistantly rank high, with none ever finishing lower than ninth place. Even the one ninth place finish came on a tract which had fifteen bids.

The lack of success of single independent bidders, and independent joint ventures is also notable, but not unexpected. Together, these two bidding types accounted for fully two-thirds of all bids placed (1835 of 2743), but won only 57 percent of the tracts (269 of 468). While single independents and independent joint ventures had similar relative success, as shown by the frequency distributions in Table 4-15a, their level of bidding was remarkably different. Table 4-15b indicates that while independent joint ventures won with an average $\ln(B)$ of 15.82 (or \$7.4 million), independent firms bidding alone averaged only 15.05 (or \$3.4 million). Extending the remarks in the previous section, this difference may be due to a tendency for independent joint ventures to bid on more valuable tracts. Table 4-16 expands Table 4-7 to include all five types of bidders. The table shows that independent joint ventures did place a much larger share of their bids on valuable tracts, as measured by number of competitors, which accounts for the fact that although their bids were higher, they were no more successful than single independents.

Rank	Pure Bidding Joint Ventures		Other Bidders			All Bidders
	Mixed J. V.	Major J. V.	Single Major	Single Indep.	Indep. J. V.	
1	.22	.50	.19	.15	.14	.17
2	.20	.13	.14	.11	.13	.14
3	.14	.10	.13	.12	.12	.13
4	.12	.05	.10	.11	.11	.11
5	.09	.08	.06	.09	.10	.09
6	.07	.00	.07	.09	.08	.08
7	.04	.03	.05	.08	.08	.07
8	.03	.08	.05	.05	.07	.05
9	.03	.03	.07	.06	.04	.05
10	.02	.00	.05	.04	.04	.04
11	.02	.00	.05	.03	.03	.03
12	.01	.00	.01	.03	.03	.02
13	.01	.00	.02	.02	.02	.02
14	.01	.00	.00$^+$	.02	.01	.01
15	.00	.00	.01	.00$^+$	.01	.00$^+$
16	.00	.00	.00	.00$^+$	.00$^+$	.00$^+$
17	.00	.00	.00	.00$^+$	.00	.00$^+$
No. of Bids	587	38	283	615	1220	2743

Table 4-15a: Frequency Distributions of Bids, By Detailed Bidder Type and Bid Rank. (Five Recent Sales.)

Rank	Pure Bidding Joint Ventures		Other Bidders			All Bidders
	Mixed J. V.	Major J. V.	Single Major	Single Indep.	Indep. J. V.	
1	15.82	15.84	15.39	15.05	15.82	15.62
2	15.56	15.18	15.20	14.67	15.27	15.24
3	15.07	15.07	14.76	14.43	15.24	14.97
4	15.09	15.45	14.84	14.30	15.03	14.87
5	15.05	15.03	14.10	14.48	14.85	14.77
6	15.32	---	14.82	14.14	14.82	14.74
7	14.75	16.54	14.42	14.37	14.87	14.69
8	15.25	15.33	14.40	14.25	14.62	14.62
9	15.55	14.95	14.40	13.72	14.56	14.46
10	14.74	---	13.35	14.09	14.95	14.47
11	15.31	---	13.43	13.79	14.71	14.38
12	14.92	---	13.32	13.47	14.58	14.20
13	15.12	---	13.74	12.96	14.52	14.05
14	14.97	---	14.23	13.03	14.00	13.84
15	---	---	13.38	13.13	14.16	13.85
16	---	---	---	10.13	14.10	12.11
17	---	---	---	10.33	---	10.33
Overall Average	15.36	15.54	14.66	14.32	15.06	14.92
No. of Bids	587	38	283	615	1220	2743

Table 4-15b: Averages of Bids by Detailed Bidder Type and Bid Rank.[a]

[a]Figures reported are averages of natural logarithms of bids.

(Tract Quality)	Pure Bidding Joint Ventures		Other Bidders			All Bidders
Number of Real-istic Bids (N)	Mixed J. V.	Major J. V.	Single Major	Single Indep.	Indep. J. V.	
(Low) $1 \leq N \leq 5$	33%	34%	26%	28%	21%	26%
(Medium) $6 \leq N \leq 10$	39%	34%	33%	40%	40%	39%
(High) $11 \leq N \leq 17$	28%	32%	41%	32%	39%	35%
No. of Bids:	587	38	283	615	1220	2743

Table 4-16: Distribution of Bids by Tract Quality, and Detailed Bidder Type.
(Five recent sales.)

Returning to Table 4-15b, note finally that the losing bids by all single firm bidders, both major and independent, were small, compared to the losing bids by other bidders. Chapter III's theory would predict exactly these results if single firm bidders had the worst exploration data of the five types, as seems likely. Because of their poor information, they have a great risk of overbidding, and therefore bid a small fraction of their estimate of tract value, to prevent overbidding.

Tables 4-17a and 4-17b expand Table 4-8 to include the five bidding sub-types. The restriction to tracts with exactly five bidders controls to some extent for variation in tract quality. Although dealing with a small sample of bids, independents bidding alone fared poorly, winning with only about nine percent of their bids (see Table 4-17a). All of the bidders involving majors, including single majors, won more than the average twenty percent of the time.

The level of bids, shown in Table 4-17b shows that winning bids were reasonably constant across bidder types, with the exception of mixed joint ventures. Also, as in Table 4-15b, the single firm bidders have relatively low losing bids.

This section has shown that the somewhat arbitrary distinction between pure bidding joint ventures and other bidders may not completely distinguish bidders with superior exploration data from those with poorer data. In particular, among those bidders classified as "other," single independent oil companies behave as though they possessed relatively poor information,

Rank	Pure Bidding Joint Ventures		Other Bidders			All Bidders
	Mixed J. V.	Major J. V.	Single Major	Single Indep.	Indep. J. V.	
1	.25	1.00	.26	.08	.19	.20
2	.25	.00	.15	.13	.23	.20
3	.21	.00	.30	.20	.17	.20
4	.15	.00	.11	.31	.21	.20
5	.15	.00	.18	.28	.20	.20
No. of Bids:	48	2	27	39	89	205

Table 4-17a: Frequency Distributions of Bids on Tracts
Receiving Exactly Five Bids, by Detailed
Bidder Type and Bid Rank.

Rank	Pure Bidding Joint Ventures		Other Bidders			All Bidders
	Mixed J. V.	Major J. V.	Single Major	Single Indep.	Indep. J. V.	
1	15.55	15.50	15.48	15.24	15.31	15.41
2	14.99	---	14.75	14.45	14.88	14.85
3	14.49	---	13.98	14.53	14.53	14.41
4	13.74	---	14.73	14.05	13.85	13.95
5	13.46	---	12.75	12.57	13.33	13.08
Overall Average:	14.62	15.50	14.34	13.88	14.37	14.34
No. of Bids	48	2	27	39	89	205

Table 4-17b: Averages of Bids on Tracts Receiving Exactly Five Bids, by Detailed Bidder Type and Bid Rank.[a]

[a]Figures reported are averages of natural logarithms of bids.

compared to both single majors, and independent joint ventures. Among pure bidding joint ventures, those consisting of only majors, while not plentiful, were amazingly successful, without appearing to have a serious overbidding problem. That is, major joint ventures win with a large share of their bids (Tables 4-15a and 4-17a), but do not pay very much more than the overall average (Tables 4-15b and 4-17b).

6. The Effects of Eliminating Pure Bidding Joint Ventures

Joint ventures have two effects on competition in offshore sales. Competition increases when firms otherwise too small to bid participate in the sales. Competition decreases, however, when firms which would otherwise bid alone form a partnership. The net effect of these two tendencies is difficult to judge, but this section will attempt to place an upper bound on the costs of prohibiting pure bidding joint ventures. That is, what if major oil companies were not allowed to enter any joint ventures for bidding.

Joint ventures encouraging small firms to participate in offshore sales are generally considered to be desirable. Any discussion of the negative impact of joint ventures on competition centers on the major oil companies, which would without doubt bid in offshore sales even if they were not permitted to form joint ventures.

The regressions in section four (Tables 4-9 through 4-14) provide a basis for estimating the impact of PBJVs on levels of all bids, and winning bids in particular. The impact on winning bids is of course of most interest, since only winning bids are paid to the government in the form of bonuses.

The extent to which government revenues would change in the absence of PBJVs depends primarily on the extent to which PBJV bids are elevated above other bids. But the disbanding of PBJVs may cause the number of bids submitted on each tract to increase. The relationship between changes in the number of bids and changes in the level of bids will be discussed shortly.

For the present, suppose that the number of bids per tract would have remained unchanged, had PBJVs not participated in the thirteen wildcat sales under study. Those bidders previously classified as PBJVs, simply place the same number of bids, but acting as some other type of bidder. This behavior could occur if firms face a constraint on the total dollar amount which they can bid in a sale. In this event, a group of firms would bid the same aggregate amount, whether they bid independently or in a partnership.

Tables 4-18 and 4-19 estimate the changes in government revenue which would have occurred in the absence of PBJVs. The tables use regression models 3 and 4 respectively to find the difference in average winning bids between PBJVs and other bidders. Table 4-18 uses model 3, in which the dependent variable was winning bid, in dollars (see Table 4-12). In this model, the difference between winning bids of PBJVs and others is simply the coefficient of the PBJV dummy variable γ_3, reported

(1)	(2)	(3)	(4)
Sale Number[a]	Number of PBJV Wins	Coefficient of PBJV Dummy[b] ($ thous.)	Change in Total Bonus in Absence of PBJVs = $-(2) \times (3)$ ($ thous.)
1	4	547	-2,188
2	13	-459	5,967
3	28	-196	5,488
4	16	-493	7,888
5	23	11	-253
6	13	-1,281	16,653
7	46	-5,498*	252,908
8	16	1,370	-21,920
9	19	-2,067	39,273
10	37	5,059	-187,183
11	34	2,263	-76,942
12	9	2,299	-20,691
13	47	5,299	-249,053

Total Change (Sum sales 1-13): -230,053

Table 4-18: Estimated Change in Government Revenue from Banning PBJVs: Model 3.

[a] See Table 4-1 for sale dates

[b] Coefficients are estimates of γ_3 from Table 4-12.

PBJV = Pure Bidding Joint Venture.

(1) Sale No.[a]	(2) No. of PBJV wins	(3) Coefficient of PBJV Dummy[b]	(4) Average $\ln$(WB) for PBJV	(5) Average $\ln$(WB) for Others	(6) Average Dollar Difference = $e(4) - e(5)$ ($ thous.)	(7) Change in Total Bonus, in Absence of PBJVs = $-(2) \times (6)$ ($ thous.)
1	4	.23	13.60	13.37	164	-656
2	13	-.18	12.47	12.65	-52	676
3	28	-.34	13.21	13.54	-219	6,139
4	16	-.38	12.53	12.91	-127	2,026
5	23	.61	13.66	13.05	394	-9,062
6	13	-.30	13.92	14.22	-395	5,132
7	46	-.97	14.19	15.16	-2,385	109,689
8	16	.43	14.68	14.25	836	-13,381
9	19	-.35	14.97	15.32	-1,317	25,031
10	37	.26	15.52	15.27	1,255	-46,449
11	34	.21	16.07	15.86	1,767	-60,062
12	9	.16	16.05	15.88	1,393	-12,534
13	47	.46	15.70	15.24	2,411	-113,308

Total Change (Sum, sales 1-13):   -106,759

Table 4-19:   Estimated Change in Government Revenue from Banning PBJVs: Model 4.

[a] See Table 4-1 for sale dates   *Significant at 5 percent level.

[b] Coefficients are estimates of δ_3 from Table 4-13. **Significant at 1 percent level.

PBJV = Pure Bidding Joint Venture.   WB = Winning Bid (in dollars).

in Table 4-18, column 3. In model 4, which was used to construct
Table 4-19, the dependent variable was the natural logarithm of
winning bid. To find the dollar difference in bids placed by
different types of bidders, it is necessary to first calculate
the average bids, shown in columns 4 and 5 of Table 4-19. The
difference between the antilogarithm of those two averages is
reported in column 5.

The estimated dollar difference between PBJV winning bids,
and the winning bids of other bidders times the number of winning
bids placed by PBJVs gives the total amount by which bonus
payments were elevated by the presence of PBJVs. The negative
of this figure indicates the fall in revenue which would occur in
the absence of PBJVs, and this figure is reported in column 4 of
Table 4-18 and column 7 of Table 4-19. Note that a positive
estimated change in revenue means that total bonus payments would
have been larger, had PBJVs not been allowed to bid.

The results vary from sale to sale, and are made somewhat
tenuous by the fact that in many instances in both models, the
coefficient of the PBJV dummy carried little statistical significance. In both cases, the sum of all the changes from the thirteen
sales is negative, indicating a fall in bonus payments in the
absence of PBJVs. The fall, however, is slight compared to the
\$8.6 billion in bonuses actually paid for wildcat tracts in the
thirteen sales. (See Table 2-1 for the actual bonus paid in each
sale.) The loss in revenue of \$230 million estimated in Table 4-18
is less than three percent of the total bonus paid.

The revised models 3' and 4', which incorporate a time variable, and were estimated using data from all thirteen sales, produce slightly different results. Table 4-20 finds that the estimate of revenue loss using model 3' is nearly eight times the estimate using model 4'. The difference occurs since the average bids calculated using model 4' are geometric averages, rather than arithmetic averages, and are consequently smaller (since large values are given less weight).

To judge the impact of PBJVs on dollars spent in offshore sales, model 3 is the better choice, since it explains dollars bid, not ℓn(dollars spent). Thus the analysis in Tables 4-18 and 4-20 (row 1) indicates that PBJVs contributed an extra 230 million to 863 million dollars to the thirteen offshore sales, or on the order of three to ten percent of the $8.6 billion spent.

If the number of bids increased as a result of the banning of PBJVs, the loss in revenue might be smaller. The losses could be reduced if increased competition for tracts resulted in higher winning bids. Table 4-2 indicated that winning bids were closely correlated with number of bids, and the coefficient on number of bids in both model 3 and 4 was always positive and highly significant.

The strong positive relationship between winning bid and number of bidders occurs at least in part since both variables are related to a third, unmeasurable variable: tract quality. According to the theory developed in Chapter III, each bidder

Model	(1) Dependent Variable	(2) Number of PBJV wins	(3) Coefficient of PBJV Dummy[a]	(4) Average ℓn(WB) for PBJV	(5) Average ℓn(WB) for Others	(6) Average \$ Difference (\$ thous.)	(7) Change in Total Bonus in Absence of PBJVs = -(2) x (6) (\$ thous.)
3'	WB	305	2828**	---	---	2828	-862,540
4'	ℓn(WB)	305	.25**	14.30	14.05	358	-109,224

Table 4-20: Estimated Change in Government Revenue from Banning PBJVs: Models 3' and 4'.

[a]Coefficients are estimates of γ_3 and δ_3 from Table 4-14.

PBJV = Pure Bidding Joint Venture

WB = Winning Bid

**Significant at the 1 percent level.

wants to avoid paying more than a tract is worth, by having his winning bids, on average, equal the true tract value, regardless of the number of opponents. Only if firms did not recognize the overbidding problem, and if they persistently placed bids equal to their full estimates of tract value, would winning bids rise as a result of additional bidders. Thus, were a ban placed on pure bidding joint ventures, and number of bidders increased as a result, the level of winning bids would not be expected to change, except during a short run adjustment period.

In practice, it is impossible to tell how much of the relation-ship between level of winning bids and number of bidders is due to their common relationship to tract quality, and to what extent winning bids on tracts of fixed quality would rise with more bids. In the face of this uncertainty, the 230 million to 863 million dollar loss in revenue can only be taken as a maximum. To the extent that (1) number of bids per tract increase, and (2) winning bids increase as a result of the increases in number of bids; the loss could be less than the figures reported.

7. The 1975 Department of Interior Policy

The previous section considered some of the effects of eliminating pure bidding joint ventures (PBJVs), defined as those joint ventures containing at least one major oil company. Recent proposals of the Department of Interior, discussed briefly in Chapter I, would not eliminate all PBJVs, but only those with two or more majors.

The original Department of Interior definition of "major oil company" classified any firm with worldwide hydrocarbon reserves in excess of the equivalent of five billion barrels of oil as a major. Under this definition, seven oil companies qualified as majors.[9] More recently, the Department has changed its definition, and now uses average daily world production as the yardstick. Any firm with average daily hydrocarbon production exceeding the equivalent of 1.6 million barrels of oil is considered a major.[10] The revised definition has the effect of including one additional company in the list of majors.[11] The seven firms classified as majors in this study correspond to the Department's original list of seven (See Table 4-3).[12]

For this section, the eighth firm, Atlantic Richfield (Arco) is excluded as a major. The exclusion of Arco as a major makes little difference to the analysis of joint ventures with two or more majors. Arco bid only eleven times with one or more of the seven other majors in all of the thirteen sales, and eight of those bids were winners. Eight of those bids, and six of the wins, however, came in the December, 1973 sale (sale number 13).

The proposed ban on joint ventures with more than two majors includes all of the category called major joint ventures in section 5 (those joint ventures with only majors as partners), and in addition some, but not all of the category called mixed joint ventures (with both major and independent members). Table 4-21 indicates the number of bids which would have been affected by such a rule in past sales. The number of major joint ventures has been declining in recent sales, but the number of mixed partnerships with two or more majors has increased. The proposed rule would have covered about eight percent of all bids, and twelve percent of all winning bids in past sales.

The Department of Interior places great stock in having a large number of bidders. In support of the proposed ban on joint ventures with more than one major, a Department spokesman has said, "When there are six bidders we do much better than when there are two bidders, regardless of who the bidders are."[13]

This emphasis on increasing the number of bidders ignores the nature of the relationship between winning bid and number of bidders. From Table 4-2, it is undeniable that a strong positive relationship exists between number of bids and winning bid. The problem lies in the direction of causation. If number of bids really causes the level of winning bids, then a policy which increases the number of bids per tract will increase government revenues. But, as pointed out in the previous section, a major reason for the correlation between number of bids and level of winning bid, is their common connection to tract quality. Therefore, since increasing the number of bidders does not increase tract quality, winning bids will not automatically rise as a result of more bidders.

Theoretically, joint ventures with two or more majors should have even better tract evaluation data than those with only one major. They should be correspondingly more confident in their

Sale No.[a]	Total No. of Bids	Bids by Major JVs[b]	Bids by Mixed JVs with ≥ 2 Majors	Total Bids Effected by USDI Rule	Total No. of Winning Bids	Total Winning Bids Effected by USDI Rule
1	327	0	0	0	90	0
2	382	42	0	42	121	11
3	414	73	2	75	147	27
4	533	36	0	36	206	14
5	661	48	0	48	205	12
6	727	50	0	50	158	8
7	160	25	48	73	71	41
8	522	33	10	43	110	13
9	928	14	0	14	119	6
10	259	10	8	18	62	12
11	684	1	20	21	116	4
12	535	5	38	43	96	6
13	337	8	77	85	75	28
All	6469	345	203	548	1576	182

Table 4-21. Number of Bids Effected by Proposed Department of
Interior Rule.

[a]See Table 4-1 for sale dates.

[b]Majors include seven largest firms.

USDI = U. S. Department of Interior.

estimates of tract value, and have less fear of overbidding. Thus, their bids in general should be even greater than those of PBJVs, although their winning bids should still average the same amount as those of other bidders.

Regression models 1' - 4' were re-estimated, using a dummy variable for joint ventures effected by the proposed Department of Interior rule, rather than for all PBJVs. Models 1" - 4" are as follows:

(1") $B = \alpha_0 + \alpha_1 N + \alpha_2 A + \alpha_3 D' + \alpha_4 Y + u_\alpha;$

(2") $\ln B = \beta_0 + \beta_1 N + \beta_2 A + \beta_3 D' + \beta_4 Y + u_\beta;$

(3") $WB = \gamma_0 + \gamma_1 N + \gamma_2 A + \gamma_3 D' + \gamma_4 Y + u_\gamma;$

(4") $\ln(WB) = \delta_0 + \delta_1 N + \delta_2 A + \delta_3 D' + \delta_4 Y + u_\delta;$

where
  B = non-winning bid (in \$ thous.);
  WB = winning bid (in \$ thous.);
  $\ln(B)$ = natural logarithm if bid (in dollars);
  $\ln(WB)$ = natural logarithm of winning bid (in dollars);
  N = number of bidders per tract;
  A = acres per tract;
  D' = dummy variable for joint ventures including two or more of the seven majors.

On losing bids, the joint ventures involving two or more majors bid an average of $e^{\hat{\beta}_3} = e^{.49}$ or 1.63 times the average losing bids of other bidders. For winning bids, on the other hand, the joint ventures with two or more majors bid $e^{\hat{\delta}_3} = e^{.17} = 1.19$ times the average winning bids of other bidders. These results tend to support the hypothesis that better information raises losing bids more than it does winning bids (see p. 126).

Because the joint ventures which fall under the proposed ban

Coefficient of Variable

Model[a]	Dependent Variable	Const.	No. of Bids	Acres	J. V. Dummy	Year	R^2	No. of Observations
1"	B	-21213	576** (26)	.246** (.100)	3182** (338)	283** (18)	.21	4893
2"	$\ell n(B)$	4.46	.18** (.005)	.00014** (.00002)	.49** (.07)	.12** (.003)	.45	4893
3"	WB	-33543	1608** (77)	.445* (.235)	4931** (794)	458** (46)	.34	1576
4"	$\ell n(WB)$	4.78	.30** (.008)	.00022** (.00002)	.17** (.08)	.11** (.005)	.66	1576

Table 4-22: Estimated Coefficients of Models 1" - 4".

[a]See text for description of models.

*Significant at 5 percent level.

**Significant at 1 percent level.

do tend to pay more for tracts which they win, winning bids can be expected to fall when the ban takes effect. The hypothetical loss for past sales is calculated in Table 4-23, following the same methods used in constract Table 4-20. The estimated loss is comparable to the loss incurred when all PBJVs were hypothetically banned.[14]

If revenues actually rise as a result of the ban, then the Department of Interior was correct in assuming that increased numbers of bidders lead to higher winning bids. At the same time, however, industry members will have to realize that they are probably paying more than the offshore tracts are worth.

One potential benefit of a ban on certain types of joint ventures not yet considered, concerns the allocation of offshore tracts among firms. One reason for permitting joint venture bidding in the first place is to enable small firms to join together to bid in offshore sales. If joint venture bidding also makes major oil companies stronger, eliminating any advantage granted to small firms, then a partial ban on joint ventures among majors, such as the one proposed, is definitely in order. In fact, major oil companies have by themselves controlled fewer and fewer of the tracts leased. Table 4-24 shows that in the three most recent sales in the analysis, majors bidding alone and major joint ventures won few, if any tracts. Rather than keep to themselves, majors have bid in mixed joint ventures more and more. In the last three sales, independents had at least some interest in 81 percent of the tracts leased!

Model	Dependent Variable	Number of Wins by Affected JVs	Coefficient Of J.V. Dummy[a]	Average $\ell n(WB)$ for JV	Average $\ell n(WB)$ for Others	Average $ Difference ($ thous.)	Change in Bonus in Absence of JVs = -(2)x(6) ($ thous.)
3"	WB	178	4931**	---	---	4931	877,718
4"	$\ell n(WB)$	178	.17**	14.25	14.08	240	- 42,726

Table 4-23: Estimated Change in Government Revenue from Banning Joint Ventures with Two or More Majors: Models 3" and 4".

[a]Coefficients from Table 4-22.

[b]Majors include seven largest firms

WB = Winning Bid.

**Significant at 1 percent level.

| | | Pure Bidding JVs | | | | | |
| | | Effected by USDI Rule | | | | | |
Sale No.[a]	Single Major	Major J. V.	Mixed JV, ≥2 Majors	Mixed JV; 1 Major	Single Indep.	Indep. J. V.	No. of Tracts
1	63%	0%	0%	4%	18%	14%	90
2	44	9	0	2	30	16	121
3	31	18	0	1	33	18	147
4	45	7	0	1	35	12	206
5	58	6	0	5	22	9	205
6	40	5	0	3	18	34	158
7	27	22	32	10	4	4	71
8	23	7	4	3	49	14	110
9	22	5	0	11	28⁻	34	119
10	24	13	7	40	8	8	62
11	6	1	2	26	22	43	116
12	3	0	6	3	6	81	96
13	3	5	32	25	31	4	75
All	33%	7%	4%	8%	25%	22%	1576

Table 4-24: Percentage of Tracts Won by Each Type of Bidder.[b]

[a]See Table 4-1 for sale dates.

[b]Majors include seven largest firms.

On the other side of the coin, majors had at least some
interest in about 55 percent of the tracts leased in those three
sales.

The Department of Interior ban might put an end to some
mixed joint ventures, and majors might bid alone again, as they
did frequently in earlier sales. Then some tracts, which otherwise
would have been won by a mixed joint venture, might be kept out
of the hands of independents. Alternatively, mixed joint ventures
with only one major may grow in popularity, continuing a trend
already taking place.

It is impossible to foresee all of the outcomes of the
proposed ban on joint ventures with two or more majors.
The U. S. Department of Interior hopes that (1) winning bids
on offshore tracts will rise, and (2) independent oil companies
will have a better chance of winning tracts. This section has
shown that the level of winning bids should not be expected to
rise, and might even fall by up to ten percent. As to the
distribution of tracts, the use of mixed joint ventures, in
which both majors and independents are members, has allowed both
types of firms to have interests in a substantial number of offshore tracts. The ban on some types of mixed joint ventures may
or may not prove beneficial to independents. If majors return to
bidding alone, independents may suffer from not being able to
share risks and costs with majors.

FOOTNOTES

1. Edward Cowan, "U. S. Plans to Prohibit Joint Bidding for Offshore Oil Leases by 8 Big Companies," The New York Times, January 5, 1975, p. 31.

2. The O.C.S. Statistical Summary can be obtained by writing to:
    U. S. Department of Interior
    Bureau of Land Management
    O.C.S. Office
    Room T-9003
    Federal Office Building
    701 Loyola Avenue
    New Orleans, Louisiana 70113.

3. Data available from the author upon request.

4. Production data for offshore tracts, through 1970, is contained in: L. K. Weaver, C. J. Jirik and H. F. Pierce, Offshore Petroleum Studies: Historical and Estimated Future Hydrocarbon Production From U. S. Offshore areas and the Impact on the On- shore Segment of the Petroleum Industry. (Information Circular 8575). (Washington: U. S. Department of Interior, Bureau of Mines, 1973). Cost estimates may be found in L. K. Weaver, H. F. Pierce and C. J. Jirik, Offshore Petroleum Studies: Composition of the Offshore U. S. Petroleum Industry and Estimated Costs of Producing Petroleum in the Gulf of Mexico (Information Circular 8557) (Washington: U. S. Department of Interior, Bureau of Mines, 1972). A method of calculating discounted present value is contained in: T. M. Garland, W. D. Dietzman and J. G. Thompson, Determining Discounted Cash Flow Rate of Return and Payout Time for Onshore Development Wells: A graphical Approach. (Information Circular 8593) (Washington: U. S. Department of Interior, Bureau of Mines, 1973).

5. "A Competitive Bidding Strategy," Operations Research, Vol. 4, No. 1 (Feb. 1956), pp. 104-112.

6. "Competitive Bidding," Operations Research Quarterly, Vol. 10, No. 1 (March, 1959), pp. 49-55.

7. Ibid., p. 51.

8. U.S. Department of Interior, "Outer Continental Shelf Lands Act: Proposal on Oil and Gas Census," Federal Register, Vol. 39, No. 80 (April 29, 1974), pp. 14511-14512.

9. Ibid., and Cowan, loc. cit.

10. U. S. Department of Interior, "Qualified Joint Bidders," Federal Register, Vol. 30, No. 36 (Feb. 21, 1975), pp. 7673-7676.

11. Cowan, loc. cit.

12. The eighth firm, Atlantic Richfield, was excluded from the list of majors used in the preceding analysis, because Atlantic Richfield has not behaved like a major, in terms of joint venture participation. The longest-lived joint venture in the federal offshore sales is the CATC group (Continental, Atlantic, Tidewater, Cities Service, with names now changed to Continental, Arco, Getty, Cities Service). All or part of the CATC group has bid together in virtually every federal sale as an exploration and bidding joint venture, not a pure bidding joint venture.

13. Darius Gaskins, quoted in Cowan, loc.cit.

14. Estimates of loss were also computed using the old Department of Interior definition of major (seven largest companies). The coefficients on the joint venture dummys in Models 3" and 4" were $\hat{\gamma}_3 = 5652$ (854) and $\hat{\delta}_3 = .22$ (.09). The corresponding estimates of change in revenue were (in \$ thous): -972,144 and -62,436 respectively. Compare these figures to Table 4-23.

CHAPTER V

CONCLUSIONS

1.   Summary of the Study

The object of this study has been to draw certain generalizations concerning the bidding behavior of joint ventures, and to empirically test those generalizations. Joint ventures are, however, difficult to characterize in general since they form for many and varied reasons. Each joint venture's behavior also depends, of course, on the characteristics of its member firms.

Joint venture bidding enables oil companies to become stronger competitors in offshore oil and gas leasing sales, through the pooling of such things as capital, information, technical knowledge and equipment, costs and risks. Joint venture bidding provides firms unwilling or unable to bid alone a means to participate in the sales. The fact that joint venture bidding has come to be used by both large and small bidders in offshore sales suggests that joint venture bidding provides benefits to even those firms which have the size and strength to bid alone.

This study has focused primarily on information pooling by joint ventures. Some partnerships represent essentially a new company formed for the purpose of exploring, bidding and operating offshore. This type of joint venture eliminates the duplication of effort which occurs when firms independently explore and evaluate offshore tracts in preparation for a sale. The amount and quality of information gathered is comparable to that gathered by a single firm acting alone. Larger and stronger firms find it unnecessary to pool exploration costs. These firms enter partnership agreements not to eliminate duplicate exploration costs, but rather to gain someone else's exploration data and interpretations. These latter ventures, which I have designated pure bidding joint ventures (PBJVs), form only shortly before a sale, and their sole objective prior to the sale is to construct bids.

Chapter III developed a theory of bidding with asymmetric information. The differences in information arose from the different types of bidders discussed above. In a preliminary model, in which all bidders had information of equal quality, the problem of overbidding was defined, and a solution proposed. Overbidding occurs when all bidders make bids equal to their (unbiased) estimate of a tract's true value. Although all estimates (and hence, bids) are unbiased, the winning bid is not unbiased, and tends to be too high. Correction for the overbidding problem is achieved by bidding less than the estimated worth of the tract. The size of the required correction depends on the accuracy, or variance of each bidder's tract evaluation, and the number of competitors.

If each bidder takes its opponents behavior as fixed, there exists a Nash, or non-cooperative equilibrium set of bids in both the symmetric and asymmetric information cases. Fear of overbidding leads sale participants to bid less than they estimate a tract to be worth, but pure bidding joint ventures, with several independent sets of exploration data, make more accurate estimates of tract value and consequently have less fear of overbidding.

The theory of bidding with asymmetric information led to three hypotheses concerning pure bidding joint ventures:

   (1) PBJVs win with a greater share of their bids than other bidders,

   (2) Average winning bids of PBJVs are the same as average winning bids of other bidders,

   (3) Average non-winning bids of PBJVs are larger than non-winning bids of other bidders.

All of these hypotheses followed from the superior information used by PBJVs in making bids.

With the record of bids kept by the U. S. Department of Interior, Chapter IV tested the three hypotheses about PBJVs, and also examined the potential costs and benefits of several policies for banning joint venture bidding, including a policy proposed by the Department of Interior, slated to take effect in mid-1975.

2. Major Findings of the Study

From interviews with representatives of the oil industry, and examination of the patterns of joint venture bidding in offshore sales, pure bidding joint ventures were defined to include all joint ventures having at least one of the seven largest oil companies as a member. Only these large companies appear willing and able to incur independent exploration costs, and furthermore the majors frequently bid with different partners. Both of these facts suggest that major oil companies enter joint ventures very near the time of a sale to share and compare exploration data.

Armed with this definition of pure bidding joint ventures,
sections four and five of Chapter IV tested the hypotheses concerning their bidding behavior. PBJVs do win with a greater percentage
of their bids than other bidders, but unexpectedly, they seem to
pay as much as 70 percent more than other bidders for tracts of
comparable quality.[1] This surprising result can be explained if
either PBJVs consistently overbid, and pay more for tracts than they
are worth; other bidders consistently underbid; or the tracts in
question are not truly of comparable value. As expected, PBJVs
had substantially higher non-winning bids than other bidders.

Using the results of the study of the impact of PBJVs on
winning bids, the estimated loss in dollars of bonus payments of
prohibiting PBJVs was placed at between two and twelve percent,
based on thirteen major wildcat sales held since 1954.[2] A similar
estimate was made of the cost of imposing the Department of Interior's
new plan to ban all joint ventures including two or more of the
largest eight oil companies. This plan would cost the government
between one and eleven percent of the bonus dollars paid.[3]

The theoretical results of the thesis raise a challenge to
the Department of Interior's contention that any policy such as a
ban on joint ventures which would increase the number of bidders per
tract, would also raise the level of winning bids. While this
study supports the Department of Interior finding of a strong
correlation between the number of bidders and the size of the winning
bid; most, if not all of the correlation results from the influence

of a third variable, tract quality, on both variables. An increase
in the number of bidders on a tract of constant quality should not
be expected to raise the winning bid substantially.

Another Department of Interior motive for proposing a ban on
certain joint ventures lies in the desire to spread offshore tracts
among a larger number of oil companies. The increasing participation
of majors in joint ventures with independents has actually led to
an increase in the number of offshore tracts shared by independents.
In early sales, when most bids were submitted by single firms,
nearly half of all tracts leased went to majors. Now, although
majors still have an interest in 51 percent of all tracts leased,
independents, through participation in joint ventures, have an
interest in over 81 percent of all tracts leased.[4]

3. Suggestions for Further Research

One shortcoming of this study lies in the treatment of tract
quality. To properly explore the relationship between number of
bidders and winning bid level requires some independent measure of
tract quality. The variable used in this study was number of bids
per tract, but this variable provided no indication of how close
winning bids were to true tract value. One possible method of
measuring true tract value, using actual production and cost
figures for each tract, was discussed in section two of Chapter IV.[5]
Using this method, after-the-fact tract values could be compared
to the actual prices paid to determine the relative success of
different types of bidders, and also to judge whether the

government receives proper payment for its resources.

A more difficult problem in the area of true tract value arises if different firms and bidders truly place different values on the same tract, because of location, respective need of crude oil, publicity, or some other reason. Under these circumstances, a model of bidding behavior becomes nearly impossible to construct, since the tract value for each firm must be included.

A second area for further research involves problems raised by constraints on the amount of capital available for bidding by any sale participant. No bidder could bid seriously on all tracts offered in a sale, but the optimal way for allocating a limited amount of capital in a sealed bid sale has not received intensive study.[6]

Questions of budget constraints within one sale lead directly to a third area needing further study: inter-temporal allocation of capital. There are a host of dynamic questions surrounding off-shore sales, particularly concerning the extent to which a firm's success in one sale effects its success in future sales. One might suspect that success in one sale might lead to slackened effort in subsequent sales, and failure in a sale would lead to renewed effort in the future. In studying this problem, however, the possibility of post-sale transactions among sale participants must be considered, since firms which win either too much or too little may adjust their offshore holdings prior to any new sales.

A fourth area of concern regarding joint venture bidding lies in what might be termed the political arena. Critics have argued that even if joint ventures do not harm competition in OCS lease sales, they do provide a forum for reaching anticompetitive agreements in areas <u>other</u> than bidding, such as marketing practices, or pricing.[7] There are certainly questions which could be raised concerning the overall impact of joint ventures on the competitiveness of the oil industry, but they are beyond the scope of this study, and may well be beyond the scope of any study.

Finally, it would be valuable to study the ultimate effect of federal offshore policies. Any government policy which made offshore sales more competitive and raised the price of leases, might simply result in higher crude oil prices. Although so far a relatively small fraction of the domestically produced oil in the United States comes from the offshore, there may already be a detectable relationship between winning bid levels and petroleum prices. There are, of course, obvious reasons to expect that oil prices will influence the level of bids, but the causation may run both ways, and bid levels, to the extent that they differ from true tract value, may exert pressure on oil prices.

FOOTNOTES

1. In model 3' of Chapter IV (see Table 4-14), the average winning bid for PBJVs was \$8,683,000 while the average winning bid for other bidders was \$5,140,000.

2. The total bonus paid in those sales was \$8.8 billion, while estimates of loss ranged between \$141 and \$1,063 million. See Tables 4-18, 4-19 and 4-20.

3. Estimates of loss range between \$70 million and \$964 million in the thirteen wildcat sales. See Table 4-23.

4. These statistics are based on the three most recent sales studied, in which 304 tracts were leased. See Table 4-24.

5. See Chapter IV, footnote 4.

6. Keith Brown recognizes the problem of capital constraints in Bidding for Offshore Oil: Toward an Optimal Strategy (Dallas: Southern Methodist University Press, 1969), p. 58. See also J. H. Griesmer and M. Shubik, "Toward a Study of Bidding Processes, Part II: Games with Capacity Limitations," Naval Research Logistics Quarterly, Vol. 10 (1963), pp. 151-173.

7. For a summary of the critics, see H. E. Leland, R. B. Norgaard and S. R. Pearson, "An Economic Analysis of Alternative Outer Continental Shelf Petroleum Leasing Policies," unpublished MS prepared for the Office of Energy R and D Policy, National Science Foundation, Berkeley, 1974, pp. 14-18.

BIBLIOGRAPHY

BOOKS

Brown, Keith C., <u>Bidding for Offshore Oil: Toward an Optimal</u>
    <u>Strategy</u>. Dallas: Southern Methodist University Press, 1969.

Christienson, Charles, <u>Strategic Aspects of Competitive Bidding</u>
    <u>for Corporate Securities</u>. Boston: Graduate School of
    Business Administration, Harvard University, 1965.

Garland, T. M., W. D. Dietzman and J. G. Thompson, <u>Determining</u>
    <u>Discounted Cash Flow Rate of Return and Payout Time for</u>
    <u>Onshore Development Wells</u>. (Information Circular 8593)
    Washington: U. S. Department of Interior, Bureau of Mines,
    1973.

Grayson, C. J., Jr., <u>Decisions Under Uncertainty: Drilling</u>
    <u>Decisions by Oil and Gas Operators</u>. Boston: Harvard
    Business School, 1960.

Kalter, R. J., W. E. Tyner and D. W. Hughes, <u>Alternative Leasing</u>
    <u>Strategies and Schedule for the Outer Continental Shelf</u>.
    Ithaca, NY: Cornell University Press, 1975.

Kaufman, Gordon M. <u>Statistical Decision and Related Techniques</u>
    <u>in Oil and Gas Exploration</u>. Englewood Cliffs, N. J.:
    Prentice Hall, 1963.

Kendall, Maurice A., <u>The Advanced Theory of Statistics</u>. Philadelphia:
    L. B. Lippincott Co., 1943.

Marks, Wayne, <u>A Survey of Leasing Procedures in Selected Foreign</u>
    <u>Countries and Selected American Coastal States</u>. Washington:
    U. S. Department of Interior, Office of Policy Analysis, 1977.

_____, <u>A Survey of Empirical Studies on the Effects of Oil and</u>
    <u>Gas Leasing Policies in Selected American Coastal States</u>.
    Washington: U. S. Dept. of Interior, Office of Policy Analysis,
    1977.

Milgrom, Paul R., The Structure of Information in Competitive Bidding. New York: Garland Publishing, Inc., 1980.

Mitchell, Edward J., ed., The Question of Offshore Oil. Washington, DC: American Enterprise Institute, 1976.

Mosteller, Frederick and R. K. E. Rourke, Sturdy Statistics: Nonparametrics and Order Statistics, Reading, Mass.: Addison-Wesley Publishing Company, 1973.

Neale, A. D., The Antitrust Laws of the United States. 2nd ed., Cambridge: Cambridge University Press, 1970.

Reece, Douglas K., Leasing Offshore Oil: An Analysis of Alternative Information and Bidding Systems. New York: Garland Publishing Inc., 1980.

Smiley, Albert K., Competitive Bidding Under Uncertainty: The Case of Offshore Oil. Cambridge, Mass.: Ballanger, 1979.

Stelzer, Irwin M., Selected Antitrust Cases: Landmark Decisions. 4th ed., Homewood, Ill.: Richard D. Irwin, 1972.

Telser, L. G., Competition, Collusion, and Game Theory. New York Aldine-Atherton, 1972.

Van Meurs, A. P. H., Petroleum Economics and Offshore Mining Legislation. New York: American Elsevier Publishing Co., Inc., 1971

Weaver, L. K., C. J. Jirik and H. F. Pierce, Offshore Petroleum Studies: Composition of the Offshore U. S. Petroleum Industry and Estimated Costs of Producing Petroleum in the Gulf of Mexico. (Information Circular 8557) Washington: U. S. Department of Interior, Bureau of Mines, 1972.

_____, Offshore Petroleum Studies: Historical and Estimated Future Hydrocarbon Production From U. S. Offshore Areas and the Impact on the Onshore Segment of the Petroleum Industry. (Information Circular 8575) Washington: U. S. Department of Interior, Bureau of Mines, 1973.

_____, Nomograph for Estimating Hydrocarbon Lease Bonus Bids in the Gulf of Mexico. (Information Circular 8609) Washington: U. S. Department of Interior, Bureau of Mines, 1973.

ARTICLES AND PERIODICALS

Arps, John J., "A Strategy for Sealed Bidding," Journal of Petroleum Technology, Vol. 17 (September, 1965), 1033-1039.

Attanasi, E. D., and S. R. Johnson, "Sequential Bidding Models: A Decision Theoretic Approach," Industrial Organization Review, Vol. 3, No. 1 (1975), 43-55.

Berg, S. V. and P. Friedman, "Causes and Effects of Joint Venture Activity: Knowledge Acquisition vs. Parent Horizontality," Antitrust Bulletin, Vol. 25, No. 2 (Spring 1980), 143-68.

Brown, Keith C., "A Note on the Apparent Bias of Net Revenue Estimates for Capital Investment Projects," Journal of Finance, Vol. 29, No. 4 (September, 1974), 1215-1216.

Capen, E.C., R. V. Clapp and W. M. Campbell, "Competitive Bidding in High Risk Situations," Journal of Petroleum Technology, Vol. 23, (June, 1971), 641-53.

Cowan, Edward. "U. S. Plans to Prohibit Joint Bidding for Offshore Leases by 8 Big Companies," The New York Times, January 8, 1975, p. 31.

Crawford, Paul B., "Texas Offshore Bidding Patterns," Journal of Petroleum Technology, Vol. 22 (March, 1970), 283-289.

Dougherty, Elmer L., and John Lohrenz, "Statistical Analysis of Solo and Joint Bids for Federal Offshore Oil and Gas Leases," Society of Petroleum Engineers Journal (April, 1978), 87-95.

_____, "Federal Offshore Oil and Gas Lease Royalty Bidding," Society of Petroleum Engineers of the AIME report no. SPEE 7400 (1978).

Dougherty, Elmer L., and M. Nozaki, "Determining Optimum Bid Fraction," Journal of Petroleum Technology (March, 1975), 349-56.

Erickson, Edward W., and Robert M. Spann, "The American Petroleum Industry," in E. W. Erickson and L. W. Waverman, eds., The Energy Question, Vol 2, North America. Toronto: Univ. of Toronto Press, 1974, 5-24.

Friedman, Lawrence, "A Competitive Bidding Strategy," Journal of the Operations Research Society of America, Vol 4, No. 1, (February, 1956).

Griesmer, J. H., and M. Shubik, "Toward a Study of Bidding Processes, Part I-III," Naval Research Logistics Quarterly, Vol. 10 (1963), 11-21, 151-173, 199-217.

_____, and R. E. Levitan, "Toward a Study of Bidding Processes, Part IV: Games with Unknown Costs," Naval Research Logistics Quarterly, Vol. 14 (1967), 415-432.

Guasch, J. L. and A. Weiss, Adverse Selection by Markets and the Advantage of Being Late," Quarterly Journal of Economics, Vol. 94, No. 3 (May 1980), 453-66.

Hammons, Lowell G., "Subsea Seismic Survey Data Aid Federal Government in Deep Water Leasing in U. S.," Offshore, Vol. 33, No. 6 (June 5, 1973), 29-31.

Hanssmann, F. and B. H. P. Rivett, "Competitive Bidding," Operations Research Quarterly, Vol. 10 (March 1959), 49-55

Hughart, David, "Informational Asymmetry, Bidding Strategies, and the Marketing of Offshore Petroleum Leases," Journal of Political Economy, Vol. 83, No. 5 (Oct., 1975), 969-985.

Johnson, Ronald N., "Auction Markets, Bid Preparation Costs and Entrance Fees," Land Economics, Vol. 55 (Aug., 1979), 313-318.

Jones, Russell O., Walter J. Mead and Philip E. Sorensen, "Free Entry into Crude Oil and Gas Production," Natural Resources Journal, Vol. 18 (October 1978), 859-876.

Kalter, R. J., T. M. Stevens and D. A. Bloom, "The Economics of Outer Continental Shelf Leasing," American Journal of Agricultural Economics, (1978), 231-288.

Klein, J. Douglass, "The Problem of Joint Ventures in Bidding for Offshore Oil," in Yakov Amihud,   ed., Bidding and Auctioning for Procurement and Allocation. New York: New York, University Press, 1976, 38-42.

Kobrin, Paul, Michael Canes and Pamela Murphy, "Is the Ban on Joint Bidding for OCS Leases by Major Oil Companies Warranted?" Critique #002, American Petroleum Institute (February 24, 1977)

Lee-Martinez, M., "Monopolization of Public Lands or Necessary Liberalization of Exploration Laws?" Natural Resource Journal, Vol. 20 No. 2 (April 1980),387-93.

Leland, H. E. "On the Existence of Optimal Policies Under Uncertainty," Journal of Economic Theory, Vol. 4 (February, 1972), 35-44.

_____, "Optimal Risk Sharing and the Leasing of Natural Resources, with application to Oil and Gas Leasing on the OCS," Quarterly Journal of Economics, Vol. 92, No. 3 (Aug., 1978), 413-437.

Logue, Dennis E., Richard James Sweeney and Thomas D. Willett, "Optimal Leasing Policy for the Development of Outer Continental Shelf Hydrocarbon Resources," Land Economics, Vol. 51, No. 3 (August 1975) 191-207.

Markham, Jesse, "The Competitive Effects of Joint Bidding by Oil Companies for Offshore Leases," in J. Markham and G. Papanek, eds., Industrial Organization and Economic Development. Boston: Houghton, Mifflin, 1970, 116-135.

Mead, Walter J., "Natural Resource Disposal Policy--Oral Auction versus Sealed Bids," Natural Resources Journal, Vol. 7 (April, 1967), 194-224.
_____, "The Competitive Significance of Joint Ventures," The Antitrust Bulletin, (Fall, 1967), 819-848.

Morris, Peter A., "Combining Expert Judgements: A Bayesian Approach," Management Science, Vol. 23, No. 7 (March 1977), 679,693.

Offshore, "Offshore Leasing Gamble--Pay Your Money and Take Your Chances," Vol. 32, No. 8 (July, 1972), p. 35.

_____, "Geophysical Program to Resume in Atlantic," Vol. 32 (July, 1972), p. 78.

Pelto, C. R., "Statistical Structure of Bidding for Oil and Mineral Rights," Journal of the American Statistical Association, Vol. 66 (September, 1971), 356-360.

Reece, Douglas K. "Competitive Bidding for Offshore Petroleum Leases," Bell Journal of Economics, Vol. 9, No. 2 (Autumn, 1978), 369-384.

_____, "An Analysis of Alternative Bidding Systems for Leasing Offshore Oil," Bell Journal of Economics, Vol. 10, No. 2 (Autumn, 1979) 659-669.

Rothkopf, Michael H., "Bidding in Simultaneous Auctions with a Constraint on Exposure," Operations Research, Vol. 25, No. 4 (July-Aug. 1977), 620-29.

_____, and Robert M. Stark, "Competitive Bidding: A Comprehensive Bibliography," Operations Research, Vol. 27 (March-April 1979), 364-390.

Smith, Benjamin T. and James H. Case, "Nash Equilibria in a Sealed Bid Auction," Management Science, Vol. 22, No. 4 (Dec. 1975), 487-97.

Smith, V. L., "Experimental Studies of Discrimination versus Competition in Sealed Bid Auction Markets," Journal of Business; University of Chicago, Vol. 40 (January, 1967), 56-84.

Stark, Robert M., "Competitive Bidding: A Comprehensive Bibliography," Operations Research, Vol. 19 (March-April, 1971), 484-490.

Sullivan B., and P. Kobrin (1978), "The Joint Bidding Ban: Pro and Anti-Competitive Theories of Joint Bidding In OCS Lease Sales," Research Paper #010, American Petroleum Institute (August 11, 1978).

Tanner, James C., "Bright Spot'--New Technique Used to Find Oil and Gas Before Drilling Wells," The Wall Street Journal, May 22, 1974, p. 1.

The Wall Street Journal, "Offshore Oil Leasing Will Surge in the 1970s Interior Department Chief Says," January 23, 1974, p. 4.

_____, "Offshore Louisiana Oil, Gas Lease Sale Nearly Doubled Usual Number of Bidders," April 1, 1974, p. 12.

_____, U. S. Rejects 23 of 114 High Bids in Oil Lease Sale," April 10, 1974, p. 2

_____, "Interior Agency to Regulate the Disclosure of Data Collected on Offshore U. S. Tracts," May 16, 1974, p. 10.

_____, "Exxon Group Hints it May Have Ended Oil Hunt Off Florida," June 11, 1975, p. 4.

Tippett, L. H. C., "On the Extreme Individuals and the Range of Samples Taken from a Normal Population," Biometrika, Vol. 17 (1925), 364-87.

Vickery, William, "Counterspeculation, Auctions, and Competitive Sealed Tenders," Journal of Finance, Vol. 16, No. 1 (March 1961), 8-37.

Wilson, Robert B., "Competitive Bidding with Asymmetric Information," Management Science, Vol. 13, No. 11 (July, 1967), 816-820.

_____, "A Bidding Model of Perfect Competition, " Review of Economic Studies, Vol. 44, No. 4 (Oct. 1977), 511-18

PUBLIC DOCUMENTS

Erickson, E. W. and R. M. Spann, "An Analysis of the Competitive Effects of Joint Ventures in the Bidding for Tracts in OCS Offshore Lease Sales," in Hearings before the Special Subcommittee on Integrated Oil Operations of the Senate Committee on Interior and Insular Affairs, Market Performance and Competition in the Petroleum Industry. (93 Congress, 2nd session, February 1974). Washington: Government Printing Office, 1974, 1691-1745.

Gaskins, D. W., Jr., and B. Vann (1975), "Joint Buying and the Seller's Return -- The Case of OCS Lease Sales," in Hearings before the Subcommittee on Monopolies and Commercial Law of the House Committee on the Judiciary, Energy Industry Investigation, Part I: Joint Ventures. (94th Congress, 1st session, July 30, 1975.) Washington: Government Printing Office, 1975, 210-220.

Mead, Walter J., "Joint Ventures -- Anti-Competitive and Pro-Competitive Effects," in Hearings before the Senate Committee on Interior and Insular Affairs, Special Subcommittee on Integrated Oil Operations, Market Performance and Competition in the Petroleum Industry, Part 3 (93rd Congress, 1st session, Dec. 12-13, 1973.) Washington: Government Printing Office, 1974, 1005-1014.

Mobil Oil Corporation (1975), "An Analysis of the Paper, 'Joint Buying and the Sellers Return -- The Case of OCS Lease Sales' by Darius W. Gaskins, Jr. and Barry Vann," in Hearings before the Subcommittee on Monopolies and Commercial Law of the House Committee on the Judiciary, Energy Industry Investigation, Part I: Joint Ventures (94th Congress, 1st session, July 30, 1975.) Washington: Government Printing Offices, 1975, 235-238.

Norgaard, R. B. "Uncertainty, Competition, and Leasing Policy," in Mason Gaffney, Oil and Gas Leading Policy: Alternatives for Alaska in 1977. a report to the State of Alaska and the Department of Natural Resources, February, 1977.

Rooney, R. F., "Profit Share Bidding for Petroleum Leases," in Mason Gaffney, Oil and Gas Leasing Policy: Alternatives for Alaska in 1977, a report to the State of Alaska and the Department of Natural Resources, February 1977.

U. S. Congress, "Outer Continental Shelf Lands Act," Public Law 212. (83rd Congress, 2nd session), 1953.

_____, "Outer Continental Shelf Lands Act Amendments of 1978," Public Law 95-372. (95th Congress, 2nd session), 1978.

_____, House, Committee on Judiciary, Subcommittee on Monopolies and Commercial Law, Energy Industry Investigation, Part I: Joint Ventures. (94th Congress, July 30, 1975 and April 14, 1976.) Washington: Government Printing Office, 1976.

_____, Senate, Committee on the Judiciary Subcommittee on Antitrust and Monopoly, Governmental Intervention in the Market Mechanism, The Petroleum Industry, Part 5: Federally Owned Oil and Gas Lands on the Outer Continental Shelf. (91st Congress, 2nd session, August 11 and 13, 1970, pursuant to Senate Resolution 40.) Washington: Government Printing Office, 1970.

_____, Senate, Committee on Interior and Insular Affairs, Outer Continental Shelf Policy Issues, Parts 1-3. (92nd Congress, 2nd session, March 23, 24, and April 11, 18, 1972, pursuant to Senate Resolution 45.) Washington: Government Printing Office, 1972.

_____, Federal Leasing and Disposal Policies. (92nd Congress, 2nd session, June 19, 1972) Washington: Government Printing Office, 1972.

U. S. Department of Interior, The Role of Petroleum and Natural Gas from the Outer Continental Shelf in the National Supply of Petroleum and Natural Gas. (Technical Bulletin 5), Washington: Government Printing Office, 1970.

_____, "Outer Continental Shelf Lands Act: Proposal on Oil and Gas Leases," Federal Register, Vol. 39, No. 80 (April 24, 1974), 14511-12.

_____, "Qualified Joint Bidders," Federal Register, Vol. 30, No. 6, (February 21, 1975), 7673-76.

_____, Bureau of Land Management, New Orleans Office, Outer Continental Shelf Statistical Summary. New Orleans: U. S. Department of Interior, Bureau of Land Management, 1975.

_____, Bureau of Land Management (1979), "Outer Continental Shelf Minerals Leasing and Rights-of-Way Granting Programs," 43 CFR Parts 2880 and 3300, in the Federal Register, Vol. 44 (June 29, 1979) 38268-38289.

_____, Geological Survey, Conservation Division, Applied Research and Analysis Section, "Production 'Lost' from Oil/Gas Reservoirs Due to Operating Costs and Royalty: Rate Sensitive Gas Reservoirs," by John Lohrenz and Ellis Monash, ARA Section Report No. 78-26 (June 26, 1976).

_____, Geological Survey, Conservation Division, Applied Research and Analysis Section, "Studies in the Relationships between Bidders' Bids, Presale Estimates, and Subsequent Production: Federal Offshore Oil and Gas Leases," ARA Section Report no. 78-32 (July 6, 1978).

_____, Geological Survey, Conservation Division (1979), LRP-5 and LPR-10 data tapes, available from John Lohrenz, Chief, Applied Research and Analysis Section, Conservation Division, MS 608, U.S. G.S., Building 85, Denver Federal Center, Denver, CO 80225.

_____, Office of OCS Program Coordination, "An Analysis of the Royalty Bidding Experiment in OCS Sale #36," mimeo, 1975.

U. S. General Accounting Office, "Outer Continental Shelf Sale No. 40 -- Inadequate Data Used to Select and Evaluate Lands to Lease," Report no. EMD-77-51, June 28, 1977.

_____, "Opportunities to resolve Some Basic Conflicts over Outer Continental Shelf Leasing and Development," Report No. EMD-78-39, March 16, 1978.

Zafren, Daniel, "An Antitrust Analysis of the Consort Provision (Sect. 17) of the 'Deep Seabed Hard Mineral Act'," in Hearings before the Senate Committee on Commerce, et al, Deep Seabed Hard Mineral Act. (94th Congress, 2nd session, May 13, 1976, Washington: Government Printing Office, 1976),185-189.

UNPUBLISHED AND OTHER SOURCES

Blitzer, David M., "An Optimal Control Analysis of Leasing Federal Oil." Unpublished Ph. D. dissertation, Columbia, 1978.

Brown, Keith C., "On Competitive Bidding Theory." Unpublished MS, Purdue University, 1973.

Cabot Consulting Group, "Competition on the Outer Continental Shelf and its Implications for Competition in Downstream Markets." Unpublished report prepared for the U. S. Dept. of Energy, Leasing Policy Development Office, July 14, 1980.

Cox, James C., "Bonus-Bid and Equity-Share OCS Leasing Policies." Processed, May, 1977.

_____, "Auction Markets in OCS oil and Gas Leases."Univ. of Arizona Working Paper, January 1979.

Engelbrecht-Wiggans, R., "A Model for the Distribution of the Number of Bidders in an Auction." Yale Univ. Cowles Foundation Disscussion Paper No. 495, Sept. 1978

_____, "Auctions and Bidding Models: A Survey." Yale University Cowles Foundation Discussion paper No. 496R, May, 1979.

Erickson, Ken, "Summary of Statistical and Economic Studies of John Lohrenz, USGS (Denver)". March 27, 1979.

Ewart, Thomas W., "Bidding for Oil Leases: A Simulation Approach." Unpublished Ph.D. dissertation, Purdue University, 1972.

Flaim, Theresa A., "The Structure of the U. S. Petroleum Industry: Concentration Vertical Integration and Joint Activities." Unpublished Ph.D. dissertation Cornell Univ., 1977.

ICF Inc., "A Preliminary Analysis of Information Asymmetry in Federal Outer Continental Shelf (OCS)Oil and Gas Lease Sales." Unpublished report to the Office of Leasing Policy Development, U.S.D.O. E., March 1979.

Johnson, Ronald N., "Competitive Bidding for Federally Owned Timber." Unpublished Ph.D. dissertation, University of Washington, 1977.

Jones, Russell O., Walter J. Meal and Philip E. Sorensen, "Economic Issues in Oil Shale Leasing Policy." Paper presented at the Oil Shale Symposium, Colorado School of Mines, Golden, Colo., April 13 1978.

_____, "Do Bidders in OCS Oil and Gas Lease Sales Behave Rationally?" Paper presented at IAEE-RFF Conference on International Energy Issues, June 5-6, 1979.

Karels, Gordon V., "Firm Behavior Under Uncertainty, The Case of OCS Petroleum Lease Sales." Unpublished Ph.D. dissertation, Purdue University, 1979.

Leland, Hayne, "Effects of Leasing Schemes on Oil Exploration." Paper presented to the NSF Conference on Econometrics and Mathematical Economics, Palo Alto, CA, May 9-11, 1975.

_____, R. B. Norgaard and Scott R. Pearson, "An Economic Analysis of Alternative Outer Continental Shelf Petroleum Leasing Policies." Unpublished MS prepared for the Office of Energy R&D Policy, National Science Foundation, Berkeley, 1974.

Mead, Walter J. and Philip E. Sorensen, "Competition and Performance in OCS Oil and Gas Lease Sales and Lease Development, 1954-1969." Final Draft Report, prepared under USGS Contract No. 14-08-0001-16552, for the Conservation Division, U.S.G.S., U. S. Department of Interior, December 31, 1979.

_____, and Russell O.Jones, "An Economic Analysis for the Performance of the Cash Bonus Bid Leasing System for OCS Oil and Gas Resources in the Gulf of Mexico." Paper presented at the Southern Economic Assoc. Annual Meeting, Atlanta, Nov. 18, 1976.

Milgrom, P. R., "A Convergence Theorem for Competitive Bidding with Differential Information." Stanford University Working Paper, September 1977.

Millsaps, Steven W. and Mack Ott, "OCS Oil Leasing, Corsortia Formation and Bidding Behavior: An Application of the Theory of Risk Aversion." presented at the American Economic Assoc. Meetings, New York, December, 1977.

_____, "Information and Bidding Behavior by Major Oil Companies for Outer Continental Shelf Leases: Is the Joint Bidding Ban Justified?" Processed, no date.

Norek, Bernard J., "Some Models of Competitive Bidding." Unpublished MS thesis, Case Institute of Technology, 1964.

Ott, Mack and Steven W. Millsaps, "Risk Aversion, Risk Sharing, and Consortium Formation: A Study of OCS Petroleum Lease Auctions." Processed, Jan. 1980.

Patterson, William E., "Sliding Scale Royalty and Offshore Lease Sale Bidding." Paper presented at the SPE-AIME Eight Hydrocarbon Economics and Evaluation Symposium, Dallas, TX, Feb. 11-13, 1979.

Pearcy, J. Rogers, U. S. Geological Survey, personal interview, December 13, 1973, with the author.

Phillips, William A., "The Performance of Joint Bidding Ventures in Competition for Outer Continental Shelf Petroleum." Unpublished Ph.D. dissertation, Florida State University, 1979.

Ramsey, James B., "Some Theoretical Results in Bidding Theory." Econometrics Workshop Paper No. 7503, Michigan State Univ., 1976.

_____, "A Summary of the Empirical Aspects of the Competitiveness of the U.S./U.K Offshore Oil Leasing Market." Hoover Occasional Paper Series No. 4, Stanford University, 1977.

_____, "Federal Off-Shore Lease Sales and a Theoretical Analysis of Alternative Bidding Procedures." Discussion Paper No. 78-08, Center for Applied Economics, Dept. of Economics, New York Univ. May, 1978.

Rankin, John, Director, Outer Continental Shelf Office of the Bureau of Land Management, U. S. Department of Interior, personal interview, December 11, 1973, New Orleans, Louisiana, with the author.

Resource Planning Association, Inc., "Analyzing Profit-Share Leasing." Prepared for the Office of Policy Analysis, U. S. Dept. of Interior, August 7, 1979.

Rose, Marshall, "The Leasing of OCS Tracts Using a Profit Sharing System." U. S. Department of Interior, Office of Policy Analysis memo, March 1977.

_____, "A Model for Computing the Expected Social Value of an OCS Sale." U. S. Department of Interior, Office of Policy Analysis memo, January 1978.

_____, "Analysis of Alternative Bid Acceptance Conditions for OCS Sales." U. S. Department of Interior, Office of Policy Analysis memo, April 1, 1978.

_____, "Reservation Prices, Fair Market Value, and Bid Acceptance Rules for Future OCS Lease Sales." U. S. Department of Interior, Office of Policy Analysis memo, November 7, 1978.

_____, and Donald Bieniewicz, "Policy Paper for Alternative OCS Leasing Arrangements." U. S. Department of Interior, Office of Policy Analysis, processed, January 1977.

Smith, James L., "Bidding Behavior for Offshore Petroleum Leases." Unpublished Ph.D. dissertation, Harvard University, 1977.

_____, "Competitive Bidding Behavior and the 'Winner's Curse'." Paper presented to ORSA/TIMS meetings, Los Angeles, November 30, 1978.

_____, "Anti-Competitive Patterns of Joint Bidding." Processed, January 16, 1979.

Spann, Robert M. and Edward W. Erickson, "Entry, Risk Sharing and Competition in Joint Ventures for Offshore Petroleum Exploration." Unpublished MS, North Carolina State University, December 10, 1975.

Teisberg, Thomas, "A Bidding Model for the Federal Oil and Gas Lease Auction." Unpublished Ph.D. dissertation, Univ. Calif. Berkeley, May, 1978.

Vann, Barry, Risk Aversion in the Bidding for Oil and Gas Leases on the Outer Continental Shelf." Unpublished Ph.D. dissertation, Univ. of Michigan, 1979.

Watkins, Thomas G., "An Analysis of Sealed Bidding Practices in a Public Sector Market." Unpublished dissertation, Iowa State University, 1979.

Wilcox., S. M., "Entry and Joint Venture Bidding in the Offshore Petroleum Industry." Unpublished Ph.D. dissertation, Univ. Calif., Santa Barbara, 1975.

Wilson, Robert B., "A Comparative Study of Cash-Bonus Bidding and Profit Share Bidding," Processed, Stanford, CA, April 9, 1976.

Zinn, C.D., W. G. Lesso, and G. R. Givens, "OILSIM: A Simulation Model for Evaluation of Alternative Bidding Procedures." Paper presented at the American Society of Mechanical Engineers Winter Annual Meeting, November 30, 1975.

APPENDIX A: AN EMPIRICAL STUDY OF OFFSHORE

LEASING SALES: AN UPDATE

This appendix updates the empirical analysis of the effects of

joint bidding in OCS sales contained in Chapter IV. In particular,

the theory developed in Chapter III suggested that bidders with better

information, identified as pure bidding joint ventures (PBJV's, see

pp. 41, 42) should:

(a)   bid with more confidence, and therefore place higher <u>losing</u>
bids than other bidders, and

(b)   seek, along with other bidders, to avoid the overbidding
problem, and therefore <u>not</u> place significantly higher <u>winning</u>
bids than other bidders.

In addition, the investigation of the effects of banning certain types

of joint ventures is also revised. A more detailed analysis of the

actual ban imposed by the U. S. Department of the Interior is contained

in Appendix B.

1.   The Revised Data Set

As does Chapter IV, this update relys on data on bonus bids placed

on wildcat tracts, and unrealistically low bids and bids rejected by

the government are excluded. All data comes from the LPR (Lease

Production and Revenue) data tapes maintained by the U. S. Geological

Survey (USGS).[1]

There are several changes and additions to the variables used in Chapter IV. First, instead of number of bids on a tract, number of realistic bids on a tract was computed, on the grounds that unrealistic bidders make little or no effort to judge tract quality. Also, as noted on p.99, one shortcoming of the original study was a weak control for tract quality. The LPR data tapes from USGS contain two variables which add to the ability to control for quality: water depth (since deeper water should imply greater exploration and development costs) and the USGS pre-sale estimate of tract value, which is used on a basis for government acceptance of a high bid.

The numbers of bids by sale date are shown in Table A-1. Also shown are the adjustments made in the data set by excluding non-wildcat, non-bonus bids, and rejected or unrealistic bids. The net number of bids remaining is 10378, from 37 sales from 1954 to 1979.

To facilitate this update analysis, the data were grouped into four time periods, as follows:

Period I: 1954 - 1966 (15 sales);

Period II: 1967 - 1971 (9 sales);

Period III: 1972 - July 1975 (11 sales); and

Period IV: December 1975 - July 1979 (14 sales).[2]

The number of observations, by period, are shown in Table A-2.

The periods are defined so that period IV begins with the first sale after the Department of the Interior implemented its ban on bidding by joint ventures with two or more majors. The effects of this ban will be studied at the end of this appendix, and in Appendix B.

Table A-1: Adjustment of Data Set.[a]

Sale Date	Total No. of Bids	No. of Wildcat Bids[b]	No. of Bonus Wildcat Bids[c]	No. of Accepted Bids	No. of Realistic Bids
10/13/54	327	327	327	327	327
11/ 9/54	90	90	90	90	90
7/12/55	384	384	384	384	382
5/26/59	23	23	23	23	23
8/11/59	45	0	0	0	0
2/24/60	444	444	444	414	414
3/13/62	538	538	538	533	533
3/16/62	666	666	666	661	661
10/ 9/62	26	0	0	0	0
5/14/63	70	70	70	69	69
4/28/64	69	0	0	0	0
10/ 1/64	223	223	223	223	223
3/29/66	64	0	0	0	0
10/18/66	79	0	0	0	0
12/15/66	7	0	0	0	0
6/13/67	742	742	742	727	727
2/ 6/68	164	164	164	160	160
5/21/68	556	556	556	522	522
11/19/68	38	0	0	0	0
1/14/69	40	0	0	0	0
12/16/69	58	0	0	0	0
7/21/70	59	0	0	0	0
12/15/70	1043	1043	1043	1020	928
11/ 4/71	33	0	0	0	0
9/12/72	324	324	324	311	259
12/19/72	690	690	690	684	684
6/19/73	551	539	539	535	535
12/20/73	373	339	339	337	337
3/28/74	402	366	366	343	343
5/29/74	352	351	351	318	318
7/30/74	57	52	52	26	26
10/16/74	387	366	309	297	297
2/ 4/75	281	273	273	228	228
5/28/75	191	158	158	137	137
7/29/75	179	152	152	138	138

(Continued; see notes at end of table.)

Table A-1 (cont.)

Sale Date	Total No. of Bids	No. of Wildcat Bids[b]	No. of Bonus Wildcat Bids[c]	No. of Accepted Bids	No. of Realistic Bids
12/11/75	166	166	166	147	147
2/18/76	81	37	37	34	34
4/13/76	244	244	244	234	233
8/17/76	410	410	410	394	394
11/16/76	117	0	0	0	0
6/23/77	424	269	269	248	248
10/27/77	240	240	142	133	133
3/28/78	99	99	99	79	79
4/25/78	283	113	113	109	109
10/31/78	62	62	62	62	62
12/19/78	288	219	219	215	215
2/28/79	73	73	73	65	65
6/29/79	112	111	111	110	110
7/31/79	316	193	193	188	188
Totals:	12490	11116	10961	10525	10378

[a] Compare with Table 4-1. Note that each column represents a further restriction of the data set.

[b] Excludes bids on drainage and development tracts.

[c] Excludes royalty bids.

Period	Total No. of Bids	No. of Wildcat Bids[b]	No. of Bonus Wildcat Bids[c]	No. of Accepted Bids	No. of Realistic Bids
I	3055	2765	2765	2724	2722
II	2733	2505	2505	2429	2337
III	3787	3610	3553	3354	3302
IV	2915	2236	2138	2018	2017
Totals:	12490	11116	10961	10525	10378

Table A-2: Adjustment of Data Set, by Period.[a]

[a] Compare with Table 4-1. Note that each column represents a further restriction of the data set.

[b] Excludes bids on drainage and development tracts.

[c] Excludes royalty bids.

2. An Analysis of Pure Bidding Joint Ventures

Table A-3 presents a first test of whether bidders with better information (PBJV's) do bid more on losing bids without over-bidding on winning bids, as predicted. Table A-3 shows the winning (and losing) frequency of PBJV's and other bidders for the four sale periods. The table also shows the average value of the natural log of winning and losing bids for each type of bidder. As noted in the text (see p. 32), bids tend to be lognormally distributed, and therefore the geometric mean is the appropriate average to consider.

Inspection of Table A-3 shows that except in period I, PBJV's unexpectedly seem to place higher winning bids than other bidders, and in all periods except IV, they have a better winning percentage, which is not surprising, given their higher bids.

As for losing bids, only in periods II and III do PBJV's exhibit their hypothesized greater confidence, by placing higher bids, even in a losing cause, than other bidders. As noted in Chapter IV (p. 115), one possible explanation for the failure of Table A-3 to support the two hypotheses concerning the bidding behavior of PBJV's might be that PBJV's bid on tracts of different quality than other bidders. Table A-4 investigates this possibility by breaking down the bids of PBJV's and other bidders according to tract quality. As in Table 4-7. the proxy for tract quality used is the number of bids received for each tract.

Table A-4 shows that PBJV's bid relatively more heavily on "low" quality tracts in periods I and II. (E.g., in period I, 75%

	Total No. of Bids	Pure Bidding Joint Ventures		Other Bidders		All Bidders	
		Freq. No. of Bids	Ave. Bid[b]	Freq. No. of Bids	Ave. Bid[b]	Freq. No. of Bids	Ave. Bid[b]
Period I:							
Winning Bids	969	.41	12.60	.35	12.91	.36	12.85
Losing Bids	1753	.59	12.50	.65	12.59	.64	12.59
All bids	2722	434	12.54	2288	12.70	2722	12.68
Period II:							
Winning Bids	458	.30	14.68	.18	14.52	.20	14.55
Losing Bids	1879	.70	14.37	.82	13.84	.80	13.89
All Bids	2337	313	14.46	2024	13.96	2337	14.02
Period III:							
Winning Bids	910	.32	15.71	.26	15.01	.28	15.24
Losing Bids	2392	.68	15.31	.74	15.04	.72	15.12
All Bids	3302	949	15.44	2353	15.03	3302	15.15
Period IV:							
Winning Bids	709	.34	15.15	.36	14.40	.35	14.64
Losing Bids	1308	.66	14.97	.64	15.01	.65	14.58
All Bids	2017	659	15.03	1358	14.79	2017	14.60
All Periods:							
Winning Bids	3046	.34	14.74	.28	14.06	.29	14.24
Losing Bids	7332	.66	14.62	.72	13.96	.71	14.10
All Bids	10378	2355	14.66	8023	13.99	10378	14.14

Table A-3: Winning and Losing Frequencies, and
Bid Averages, by Bidder Type.[a]

[a]Compare with Tables 4-5 and 4-6.

[b]Figures reported are averages of natural logarithms of bids.

	Tract Quality[a]	Distribution of Bids by:		
		Pure Bidding Joint Ventures	Other Bidders	All Bidders
Period I:	Low	75.1%	62.0%	64.1%
	Medium	24.2	35.2	33.4
	High	0.7	2.8	2.5
	Total # of bids:	434	2288	2722
Period II:	Low	46.6%	30.5%	32.6%
	Medium	29.7	36.2	35.3
	High	23.6	33.3	32.0
	Total # of bids:	313	2024	2337
Period III:	Low	46.4%	45.9%	46.0%
	Medium	38.0	36.3	36.8
	High	15.6	17.8	17.2
	Total # of bids:	949	2353	3302
Period IV:	Low	49.6%	63.3%	58.8%
	Medium	47.0	31.7	36.7
	High	3.3	5.0	4.5
	Total # of bids:	659	1358	2017
All Periods:	Low	52.6%	49.5%	50.2%
	Medium	36.9	35.2	35.6
	High	10.5	15.3	14.2
	Total # of bids:	2355	8023	10378

Table A-4: Distribution of Bids by Tract
Quality.

[a]As in Table 4-7, tract quality is measured by number of bids
received on the tract, as follows: tracts receiving one to five
bids were judged low quality; six to 10 bids, medium quality,
and 11 or more bids, high quality.

of PBJV bids were on low quality tracts vs. only 62% of other bids.) In period III the distributions were very nearly the same, while in period IV, PBJV s placed a significantly _lower_ percentage of bids on "low" quality tracts.

The trend by PBJV s, toward placing bids on relatively more valuable (or at least more highly contested) tracts suggests why in Table A-3, PBJV's winning bids are below winning bids of other bidders in period I, but exceed winning bids of other bidders in later periods. By period IV, PBJV's average winning bids are much higher than winning bids of other bidders.

To try to avoid the problem of difference in tract quality, Table A-5 concentrates on tracts receiving exactly five bids. Table A-5 again shows PBJV s winning with a consistently higher proportion of their bids than other bidders. In periods II and III, however, PBJVs still show their unexpected tendency to pay relatively more for tracts which they win.

Table A-5 also shows that in all periods, as hypothesized, PBJV's place higher losing bids than do other bidders, although in periods I and III the differences are slight.

A more precise way of analyzing the behavior of PBJV s uses a regression analysis which seeks to explain the levels of winning and losing bids in terms of tract quality, and the degree of information possessed by bidders.

Tract quality was measured in Chapter IV by number of bidders, and acres in the tracts. In this revision, quality is measured by the

	Total No. of Bids	Pure Bidding Joint Ventures		Other Bidders		All Bidders	
		Freq. No. of Bids	Ave. Bid[b]	Freq. No. of Bids	Ave. Bid[b]	Freq. No. of Bids	Ave. Bid[b]
Period I:							
Winning Bids	62	.23	13.74	.20	14.03	.20	13.98
Losing Bids	248	.77	12.64	.80	12.49	.80	12.51
All Bids	310	40	12.89	270	12.79	310	12.80
Period II:							
Winning Bids	38	.22	16.18	.20	15.04	.20	15.25
Losing Bids	152	.78	14.96	.80	13.40	.80	13.65
All Bids	190	32	15.23	158	13.72	190	13.97
Period III:							
Winning Bids	51	.35	16.11	.14	15.64	.20	15.88
Losing Bids	204	.65	14.65	.86	14.58	.80	14.59
All Bids	255	75	15.16	180	14.73	255	14.85
Period IV:							
Winning Bids	38	.25	15.78	.17	16.02	.20	15.91
Losing Bids	152	.75	14.62	.83	14.18	.80	14.32
All Bids	190	68	14.91	122	14.49	190	14.64
All Periods:							
Winning Bids	189	.27	15.66	.18	14.90	.20	15.14
Losing Bids	756	.73	14.30	.82	13.50	.80	13.67
All Bids	945	215	14.67	730	13.75	945	13.96

Table A-5: Winning and Losing Frequencies, and
Bid Averages, by Bidder Type,
for Tracts Receiving Five Realistic Bids.[a]

[a]Compare with Table 4-8.

[b]Figures reported are averages of natural logarithms of bids.

number of _realistic_ bids received on a tract, acres, and two additional variables: water depth, and the U. S. Geological Survey's (USGS's) pre-sale estimate of a tract's worth.

Number of bids was replaced by number of _realistic_ bids ($\ln$ (Bid) > 10; see p. 99) on the grounds that unrealistically low, or "noise" bids were not placed based on any estimate of the worth of a tract. Water depth was included as an attempt to measure the exploration and development costs of a tract, which should be negatively related to the amount a company is willing to spend on acquiring a tract. Finally, USGS pre-sale estimate provided an independent estimate of a tract's worth, and is a figure used by the government in deciding whether to accept or reject the high bid on a tract.

Unfortunately, the LPR tapes provided by the USGS do not contain depth and pre-sale estimate data for all tracts. Table A-6 shows the availability of this data, and the regression models reported in the rest of this appendix were designed to take advantage of the data available.

Four general models, following the four in chapter IV (pp. 119-128), are estimated. the models are:

(A1) $\quad LB = \alpha_0 + \alpha_1 NR + \alpha_2 A + \alpha_3 DEPTH + \alpha_4 PRE + \alpha_5 D + \alpha_6 Y + U_\alpha$

(A2) $\quad \ln(LB) = \beta_0 + \beta_1 NR + \beta_2 A + \beta_3 DEPTH + \beta_4 \ln(PRE) + \beta_5 D + \beta_6 Y + U_\beta$

(A3) $\quad WB = \gamma_0 + \gamma_1 NR + \gamma_2 A + \gamma_3 DEPTH + \gamma_4 PRE + \gamma_5 D + \gamma_6 Y + U_\gamma$

(A4) $\quad \ln(WB) = \delta_0 + \delta_1 NR + \delta_2 A + \delta_3 DEPTH + \delta_4 \ln(PRE) + \delta_5 D + \delta_6 Y + U_\delta$

Where LB = Losing bid,
       NR = Number of realistic bids,
       A = Acres,
       DEPTH = Water depth, in feet,
       PRE = USGS pre-sale estimate,
       D = PBJV dummy (1 = PBJV bid),
       Y = Trend variable (last two digits of year),

(1)	(2)	(3)	(4)	(5)
			Bids with	
	Adjusted	Bids with	Pre-sale	Bids with
	Number of	Depth	Estimate	Both
Period	Bids[a]	Data	Data	(3) and (4)
I	2722	2722	0	0
II	2337	2334	1308	1308
III	3302	3302	3013	3013
IV	2017	808	2017	808
Totals:	10378	9166	6338	5129

Table A-6: Data Availability by Period.

[a]From Table A-2.

WB = Winning bid,

ℓn = Natural logarithm,

U_{α}, U_{β}, U_{γ}, U_{δ} = Disturbance terms

The hypotheses regarding the bidding behavior of PBJV s hold that in models A1 and A2, the coefficients on D should be positive. That is, PBJV s place higher losing bids, due to their more accurate estimate of tract value, and their reduced fear of over-bidding. In models A3 and A4, the coefficients on D should be zero if PBJV s pay no more for tracts of equal quality than other bidders.

Tables A-7 through A-10 present estimates of models A1 - A4 for each period, and for all periods. Note that due to data limitations, PRE was omitted from the period IV regressions. Two regressions were run including data from <u>all</u> periods, once <u>with</u> DEPTH and PRE (on a much reduced data set), and once without either of those variables.

The results of models A1 and A2 (Tables A-7 and A-8) indicate the following:

- NR, the number of realistic bids, as expected, has a positive and significant coefficient in every regression.

- ACRES has the expected positive and significant coefficient only in periods I and II (in both models A1 and A2) and in the regression involving all periods (in models A2 only).

- DEPTH proves to be a very poor predictor of losing bid level, having the expected significant negative sign only in period I, although negative (but not significant) in several other regressions. One possible explanation for the poor performance of Depth is that, after period I, more valuable tracts were only available in deeper water.

- PRE, the USGS pre-sale estimate of tract value (in model A1) and its natural log (in model A2) are positive and significant in all regressions where this variable was included, as expected.

- Y, the trend variable, in all regressions except those for periods I and II, had positive and significant coefficients, as expected.

Period	Constant	Number of Realistic Bids	Acres	Water Depth	Pre-Sale Estimate	PBJV Dummy	Trend	R^2	Number of Observations
I	-81	195** (11)	.115** (.026)	-1.56** (.57)	---	248** (77)	-12 (10)	.18	1753
II	9790	294** (29)	.414** (.107)	-.812 (.820)	---	2143** (299)	-174** (81)	.08	1877
III	-91418	1169** (63)	-.596** (.287)	-.015 (1.337)	.499** (.032)	3444** (458)	1273** (229)	.28	2218
IV	-70093	1155** (91)	-.096 (.390)	---	.271** (.024)	3166** (558)	871** (229)	.25	1308
All	-22925	738** (26)	.047 (.103)	---	---	3398** (226)	306** (15)	.19	7332
All	-47667	803** (42)	-.050 (.177)	.614 (.997)	.379** (.019)	3044** (341)	624** (70)	.25	3886

Table A-7: Estimated Coefficients of Model A1.[a]

$$LB = \alpha_0 + \alpha_1 NR + \alpha_2 A + \alpha_3 DEPTH + \alpha_4 PRE + \alpha_5 D + \alpha_6 Y + u_\alpha .$$

(Standard errors of estimate in parentheses.)

[a] For variable definitions, see text.

* Significant at the 5% level.

** Significant at the 1% level.

Period	Constant	Number of Realistic Bids	Acres	Water Depth	ℓn of Pre-Sale Estimate	PBJV Dummy	Trend	R^2	Number of Observations
I	12.33	.25** (.01)	.00017** (.00002)	-.00095* (.00054)	---	.13* (.07)	-.031** (.009)	.28	1753
II	13.47	.16** (.01)	.00024** (.00003)	-.00011 (.00024)	---	.68** (.09)	-.033 (.024)	.22	1877
III	4.15	.16** (.01)	-.00001 (.00003)	.00052** (.00015)	.23** (.02)	.34** (.05)	.086** (.026)	.35	2218
IV	3.20	.24** (.01)	-.00011** (.00005)	---	.16** (.02)	.41** (.08)	.105** (.031)	.33	1308
All	4.64	.20** (.004)	.00006** (.00002)	---	---	.45** (.03)	.110** (.002)	.43	7332
All	-.91	.14** (.01)	.00008** (.00002)	.00090** (.00014)	.28** (.01)	.42** (.05)	.135** (.006)	.33	3886

Table A-8: Estimated Coefficients of Model A2.[a]

$$\ell n(LB) = \beta_0 + \beta_1 NR + \beta_2 A + \beta_3 DEPTH + \beta_4 \ell n(PRE) + \beta_5 D + \beta_6 Y + u_\beta.$$

(Standard errors of estimate in parentheses.)

[a] For variable definitions, see text.
* Significant at the 5% level.
** Significant at the 1% level.

Period	Constant	Number of Realistic Bids	Acres	Water Depth	Pre-Sale Estimate	PBJV Dummy	Trend	R^2	Number of Observations
I	-1358	524** (20)	.139** (.042)	-.15 (.72)	---	-219* (120)	5.88 (15.37)	.42	969
II	11311	1154** (104)	.821** (.315)	-7.43** (3.34)	---	1120 (907)	-215 (335)	.25	457
III	-68563	3043** (176)	.036 (.576)	3.25 (2.57)	1.01** (.11)	5443** (1059)	862 (511)	.47	795
IV	-68126	3165** (177)	-1.161** (.512)	---	.60** (.06)	1438* (858)	926** (314)	.50	709
All	-31307	2234** (65)	.011 (.199)	---	---	3655** (453)	418** (29)	.34	3046
All	-57854	2320** (122)	-.053 (.398)	1.82 (2.08)	.85** (.07)	4224** (827)	748** (184)	.42	1243

Table A-9: Estimated Coefficients of Model A3.[a]

$$WB = Y_0 + Y_1 NR + Y_2 A + Y_3 DEPTH + Y_4 PRE + Y_5 D + Y_6 Y + u_Y.$$

(Standard errors of estimate in parentheses.)

[a] For variable definitions, see text.

* Significant at the 5% level.

** Significant at the 1% level.

Period	Constant	Number of Realistic Bids	Acres	Water Depth	ln of Pre-Sale Estimate	PBJV Dummy	Trend	R^2	Number of Observations
I	12.02	.43** (.01)	.00015** (.00003)	.00029 (.00051)	---	-.32** (.09)	-.017 (.011)	.50	969
II	5.48	.25** (.01)	.00035** (.00004)	.00012 (.00044)	---	.05 (.12)	.090** (.044)	.55	457
III	17.63	.22** (.01)	-.00008** (.00004)	.00053** (.00018)	.34** (.02)	.50** (.07)	-.10** (.04)	.62	795
IV	2.26	.36** (.02)	-.00022** (.00006)	---	.30** (.03)	.34** (.10)	.11** (.04)	.53	709
All	5.42	.36** (.01)	.00001 (.00002)	---	---	.28** (.05)	.11** (.003)	.57	3046
All	4.26	.21** (.01)	.00002 (.00003)	.00064** (.00016)	.40** (.02)	.45** (.06)	.058** (.014)	.60	1243

Table A-10: Estimated Coefficients of Model A4.[a]

$$\ell n(WB) = \delta_0 + \delta_1 NR + \delta_2 A + \delta_3 DEPTH + \delta_4 \ell n(PRE) + \delta_5 D + \delta_6 Y + u_\delta.$$

(Standard errors of estimate in parentheses.)

[a] For variable definitions, see text.

* Significant at the 5% level.

** Significant at the 1% level.

- Periods I and II include sales prior to 1972, and it should be noted that significant oil price inflation had not yet occurred. This may explain why bids did not rise over time in those earlier periods.

- Finally, the coefficients on D, the pure bidding joint venture dummy is, as expected, positive and significant in every regression. That is, on tracts of similar quality, PBJV s placed significantly higher losing bids than other bidders, as would be expected if these bidders had less fear of over-bidding due to their superior information on tract value.

Turning to models A3 and A4 [Tables A-9 and A-10], in which the dependent variables were winning bid and the natural log of winning bid, respectively:

- The coefficients on NR, ACRES, DEPTH, and PRE closely follow the pattern in models A1 and A2 (see above).

- The trend variable is positive and significant in model A3 only in period IV and the regressions for all periods. In model A4, period II as added to this list.

- Finally, the coefficients on PBJV only partly agree with the hypothesis that they should be zero. In period I, in both models, the coefficients are actually negative, suggesting that PBJV s win with lower bids than other bidders in that period. In periods III, IV, and the regression on all periods, however, the coefficients on PBJV are significantly positive, although they tend to be smaller than the corresponding coefficients in models A1 and A2.

In summary, the results shown in Tables A-7 to A-10 agree well with the earlier results reported in Tables 4-9 to 4-14. The sales used in Chapter IV fell in periods I, II and the early part of III. Periods I and II do support both of the hypotheses concerning PBJV s. They place higher losing bids, but not higher winning bids. Periods III and IV, however, seem to reflect the latter hypothesis, since PBJV s seem to place higher winning bids also. One possible explanation for this is that the members of PBJV s, which include one or more majors, have valued oil more highly than other bidders. As was noted at p. 104, no explicit attempt has been made to determine whether any tract in particular, or even all tracts in general, might be inherently more valuable to one bidder than to another.

A second explanation of why PBJV s might be paying more for tracts won in periods III and IV might be that they have better (lower cost) access to the physical and financial resources necessary to rapidly explore and develop offshore lands. Data necessary to test this conjecture, namely the schedule of exploration, development, and production on leased tracts, is available on the LPR data tapes. If PBJV s or some subset of them, are able to more rapidly exploit tracts leased, or have a lower proportion of dry holes, then they would be in fact justified in paying higher prices.

3. Different Types of Bidders

Following Chapter IV, greater insight can be gained into bidding behavior by breaking down bidders into five categories. Recall that pure bidding joint ventures include all consortia with one or more majors. In this section, PBJV s are disaggregated into joint ventures with two or more majors, and those with exactly one major.[3] Other bidders are broken into three categories: joint ventures with no majors, and sale bids by majors and by non-majors.

Table A-11 expands Table A-3, reports winning and losing frequencies, and the geometric average bids by these five bidder types, for the four time periods under consideration. Several interesting facts emerge from Table A-11:

	Total No. of Bids	PBJV's JV's, 2+ Majors		JV's, 1 Major		JV's, 0 Majors		Solo Major		Solo Non-Major		All Bidders	
		Freq. # of Bids	Ave. Bid[b]	Freq. # of Bids	Ave. Bid[b]	Freq. # of Bids	Ave. Bid[b]	Freq. # of Bids	Ave. Bid[b]	Freq. # of Bids	Ave. Bid[b]	Freq. # of Bids	Ave. Bid[b]
Period I:													
Winning Bids	969	.37	12.71	.47	12.49	.26	13.47	.40	12.75	.32	12.95	.36	12.85
Losing Bids	1753	.63	12.85	.53	11.93	.74	12.92	.60	12.47	.68	12.56	.64	12.59
All Bids	2722	254	12.80	180	12.19	420	13.06	1130	12.58	738	12.68	2722	12.68
Period II:													
Winning Bids	458	.37	14.67	.21	14.70	.14	14.80	.24	14.86	.19	13.85	.20	14.55
Losing Bids	1879	.63	14.29	.79	14.44	.86	14.01	.76	14.00	.81	13.43	.80	13.89
All Bids	2337	177	14.43	136	14.49	842	14.12	566	14.20	616	13.51	2337	14.02
Period III:													
Winning Bids	910	.37	16.25	.31	15.46	.21	15.51	.41	14.43	.25	14.79	.28	15.24
Losing Bids	2392	.63	15.52	.69	15.24	.79	15.27	.59	14.70	.75	14.74	.72	15.12
All Bids	3302	268	15.79	681	15.31	1297	15.32	439	14.59	617	14.75	3302	15.15
Period IV:													
Winning Bids	709	--	--	.33	15.15	.27	14.49	.44	14.32	.39	14.41	.35	14.64
Losing Bids	1308	--	--	.67	14.97	.73	14.54	.56	14.55	.61	13.98	.65	14.58
All Bids	2017	0	--	659	15.03	531	14.53	421	14.45	406	14.15	2017	14.60
All Periods:													
Winning Bids	3046	.37	14.55	.33	14.83	.20	14.81	.37	13.67	.28	13.89	.29	14.24
Losing Bids	7332	.63	14.23	.67	14.77	.80	14.48	.63	13.54	.72	13.60	.71	14.10
All Bids	10378	699	14.35	1656	14.79	3090	14.55	2556	13.59	2377	13.68	10378	14.14

Table A-11: Winning and Losing Frequencies, and Averages, by Detailed Bidder Type.[a]

[a] Compare with Tables 4-15a and 4-15b.

[b] Average bid figures reported are averages of natural logarithms.

- Solo bidders in general, and solo majors in particular tend to average the lowest winning bids, although solo majors have a surprisingly high winning percentage, over all winning on 37% of their bids. One explanation for the success of solo majors, even with relatively low bids, is that majors, through their joint ventures contacts, may learn where other firms intend to bid, and can thus avoid competition when placing solo bids. This has been called the "information hypothesis", and is explored in detail in Appendix B.

- The worst performers, in terms of winning frequency, are joint ventures with no majors, with only a 20% winning percentage. This despite the fact that their average bids are in fact <u>higher</u> than most other types of bidders. Such a result would suggest that this type of bidder consistently bids on more valuable tracts (this would account for their higher bids, but fewer wins).

- Finally, joint ventures with two or more majors show a consistent, strong ability to win tracts with a 37% winning percentage in each period, and bids that are nearly always above average, particularly in period III, immediately prior to the ban on such joint ventures.

Table A-12 expands Table A-4, and breaks down the bids by each of the five bidding types according to tract quality. As surmised, joint ventures with no majors did indeed tend to bid on tracts with more competition (i.e., more valuable tracts) in all four periods. Solo majors seemed to have faced the least competition, indicating either that they bid on less valuable tracts, or that they were able to avoid some competition. Again, these issues will be explored in Appendix B. The distribution of bids by other types of bidders are roughly similar.

As was done in Table A-5, Table A-13 attempts to minimize variation in tract quality by restricting attention to tracts receiving exactly five realistic bids. Again, winning and losing frequencies, and the geometric averages of winning and losing bids are reported, by the five bidder types. The strong showing of joint ventures with two or more majors, and the relatively weak showing of both solo

Distribution of Bids by:

| Tract Quality[a] | PBJV's | | | Solo Major | Solo Non-Major | All Bidders |
	JV's, 2+ Majors	JV's, 1 Major	JV's, 0 Majors			
Period I:						
Low	67.7%	85.6%	49.0%	70.0%	57.2%	64.1%
Medium	31.5	13.9	47.6	27.9	39.3	33.4
High	0.8	0.6	3.3	2.1	3.5	2.5
Tot. # Bids	254	180	420	1130	738	2722
Period II:						
Low	50.3%	41.9%	27.4%	30.7%	34.4%	32.6%
Medium	28.8	30.9	38.5	36.2	33.1	35.3
High	20.9	27.2	34.1	33.0	32.5	32.0
Tot. # Bids	177	136	842	566	616	2337
Period III:						
Low	41.8%	48.2%	35.8%	69.2%	50.6%	46.0%
Medium	42.5	36.3	40.2	23.9	36.8	36.8
High	15.7	15.6	24.1	6.8	12.6	17.2
Tot. # Bids	268	681	1297	439	617	3302
Period IV:						
Low	---	49.6%	54.2%	68.2%	70.0%	58.8%
Medium	---	47.0	38.2	28.5	26.6	36.7
High	---	3.3	7.5	3.3	3.4	4.5
Tot. # Bids	0	659	531	421	406	2017
All Periods:						
Low	53.4%	52.3%	38.5%	60.9%	51.7%	50.2%
Medium	35.1	37.7	33.8	29.1	34.9	35.6
High	11.6	10.0	21.1	10.0	13.4	14.2
Tot. # Bids	699	1656	3090	2556	2377	10378

Table A-12: Distribution of Bids by Tract Quality, Period, and Detailed Bidder Type.

[a]Low quality tracts received one to five bids, medium quality tracts received six to 10 bids, high quality tracts received 11 or more bids. See Tables A-4 and 4-16.

	Total No. of Bids	PBJV's JV's, 2+ Majors Freq. # of Bids	Ave. Bid[b]	JV's, 1 Major Freq. # of Bids	Ave. Bid[b]	JV's, 0 Majors Freq. # of Bids	Ave. Bid[b]	Solo Major Freq. # of Bids	Ave. Bid[b]	Solo Non-Major Freq. # of Bids	Ave. Bid[b]	All Bidders Freq. # of Bids	Ave. Bid[b]
Period I:													
Winning Bids	62	.13	13.59	.31	13.93	.20	14.16	.19	13.95	.20	14.05	.20	13.98
Losing Bids	248	.82	12.79	.69	12.27	.80	12.50	.81	12.54	.80	12.40	.80	12.51
All Bids	310	27	12.94	13	12.78	55	12.83	130	12.81	85	12.73	310	12.80
Period II:													
Winning Bids	38	.26	16.75	.15	14.73	.19	14.98	.28	15.15	.12	14.93	.20	15.25
Losing Bids	152	.74	14.90	.85	15.03	.81	13.62	.72	13.37	.88	13.09	.80	13.65
All Bids	190	19	15.39	13	14.98	70	13.87	47	13.86	41	13.31	190	13.97
Period III:													
Winning Bids	51	.46	16.24	.29	16.03	.12	15.61	.28	15.81	.06	15.20	.20	15.88
Losing Bids	204	.54	14.43	.71	14.73	.88	14.56	.72	4.66	.94	14.57	.80	14.59
All Bids	255	24	15.26	51	15.11	97	14.69	36	14.98	47	14.61	255	14.85
Period IV:													
Winning Bids	38	---	---	.25	15.78	.13	16.39	.22	15.62	.18	16.12	.20	15.91
Losing Bids	152	---	---	.75	14.62	.87	14.28	.78	14.31	.82	13.85	.80	14.32
All Bids	190	0	---	68	14.91	53	14.56	36	14.60	33	14.26	190	14.64
All Periods:													
Winning Bids	189	.30	15.73	.26	15.63	.16	15.18	.22	14.80	.15	14.70	.20	15.14
Losing Bids	756	.70	13.83	.74	14.49	.84	13.88	.78	13.23	.85	.3.31	.80	13.67
All Bids	945	70	14.40	145	14.79	275	14.08	249	13.58	206	13.52	945	13.96

Table A-13: Winning and Losing Frequencies, and Bid Averages, by Detailed Bidder Type, for Tracts Receiving Five Realistic Bids.[a]

[a]Compare with Tables 4-17a adn 4-17b.

[b]Average bid figures reported are averages of natural logarithms.

non-majors, and joint ventures with no majors show up clearly in Table A-13, particularly in period III, when joint ventures with two or more majors won with 46% of their bids, while the other two categories won with 12% and 6% of their bids, respectively. This kind of performance undoubtedly aided the decision to ban bidding by consortia of the former type.

4. The Effects of the 1975 Department of Interior Bidding Ban

The final part of this appendix contains a re-calculation of the anticipated dollar losses to the government due to a ban on joint ventures containing two or more majors. The theory in Chapter III led to the hypothesis that all bidders, regardless of the quality of their information, should construct their bids so that they, on average, pay true value when they win. Nevertheless, both Chapter IV, and this appendix suggest that PBJV s, and more specifically joint ventures of the type affected by the 1975 ban (those with two or more of the seven majors) do in fact pay more when they win. Thus, eliminating such bidders could result in a reduction in the amount received by the government, unless the ban results in a corresponding increase in the level of competition.

Following the method of Chapter IV, regression models A3 and A4 were re-estimated, using a different dummy variable. Instead of a dummy for PBJV s, the revised models, A3' and A4', use a dummy for bids that would have been banned by the 1975 USDI rule. The models were established for periods I - III, and for all periods, and the estimated coefficients are presented in Tables A-14 and A-15.

It is interesting to compare the results of models A3' and a4' to those of A3 and A4. In every case, the coeffieicnt on the dummy for a partnership with two or more majors (models A3' and A4') are greater than the corresponding coefficients on the PBJV dummy in models A3 and A4. That is in every case, ceteris paribus joint ventures with two or more majors place even higher winning bids than other PBJV s (i.e., joint ventures with exactly one major). Other coefficients in models A3' and A4' are remarkably similar to those in A3 and A4.

Table A-16 indicates the degree to which bonus bids would have been hypothetically reduced in periods I - III had the joint bidding ban been in effect in those periods.

The calculations in Table A-16 indicate that the potential loss in revenue varies widely in the three periods, and also depends on which model is used for the estimate. In period I, according to both models A3' and A4', joint ventures with two or more majors actually paid less for tracts they won, so banning them would have raised total bonus payments. By contrast in period III, those joint ventures paid dramatically more for tracts they won, and banning them, using the figures from model A3' would have reduced bonus payments by nearly 12%.[4]

The hypothetical losses for periods I - III computed in Table A-16 are very close to those computed in Chapter IV, Table 4-23 (p. 150). In the 13 sales studied in Chapter IV, there were 178 tracts won by joint ventures that would have been affected by the ban, and the estimated loss in bonus revenue was $43 million to $878 million,

Period	Constant	Number of Realistic Bids	Acres	Water Depth	Pre-Sale Estimate	Major JV Dummy	Trend	R^2	Number of Observations
I	-1146	523** (20)	.129** (.042)	-.077 (.724)	---	-11.6 (153.6)	2.45 (15.31)	.42	969
II	8236	1154** (104)	.782** (.313)	-7.05** (3.31)	---	2283** (1032)	-170 (334)	.26	457
III	-76494	2952** (174)	-.266 (.568)	3.25 (2.53)	1.03** (.11)	11915** (1649)	1002** (504)	.48	795
IV	-62706	3199** (176)	-1.188** (.512)	---	.61** (.06)	No Var.	862** (312)	.50	709
All	-34511	2225** (66)	.018 (.199)	---	---	5627** (713)	471** (29)	.34	3046
All	-74795	2268** (120)	-.284 (.391)	2.07 (2.05)	.89** (.06)	12111** (1411)	1002** (180)	.44	1243

Table A-14: Estimated Coefficients of Model A3'. [a]

$$WB = \gamma_0 + \gamma_1 NR + \gamma_2 A + \gamma_3 DEPTH + \gamma_4 PRE + \gamma_5 D' + \gamma_6 Y + u_\gamma.$$

(Standard errors of estimates in parentheses.)

[a] For variable definitions, see text

* Significant at the 5% level.

** Significant at the 1% level.

Period	Constant	Number of Realistic Bids	Acres	Water Depth	ln of Pre-Sale Estimate	Major JV Dummy	Trend	R^2	Number of Observations
I	12.39	.43** (.01)	.00013** (.00003)	.00050 (.00052)	---	-.23** (.11)	-.023** (.011)	.50	969
II	5.33	.25** (.01)	.00035** (.00004)	.00014 (.00044)	---	.12 (.14)	.092** (.044)	.55	457
III	17.93	.22** (.01)	-.00009** (.00004)	.00051** (.00018)	.34** (.02)	.59** (.12)	-.11** (.04)	.61	795
IV	3.59	.36** (.02)	-.00023** (.00006)	---	.30** (.03)	No Var.	.095** (.035)	.52	709
All	5.21	.36** (.01)	.00001 (.00002)	---	---	.32** (.08)	.11** (.003)	.57	3046
All	2.55	.21** (.01)	.00001 (.00003)	.00067** (.00016)	.40** (.02)	.73** (.11)	.082** (.014)	.60	1243

Table A-15: Estimated Coefficients of Model A4'.[a]

$$\ln(WB) = \delta_0 + \delta_1 NR + \delta_2 A + \delta_3 DEPTH + \delta_4 \ln(PRE) + \delta_5 D' + \delta_6 Y + u_\delta.$$
(Standard errors of estimate in parentheses.)

[a]For variable definitions, see text.

* Significant at the 5% level.

** Significant at the 1% level.

(1)	(2)	(3)	(4)	(5)	(6)	(7)	(8)	(9)	(10)
		No. of Major JV Wins [a]	Coefficient of Major JV Dummy	Average ln(WB) for Major JV's	Average of ln(WB) for Others	Average Dollar Difference ($ thou)	Change in Bonus Payments ($ mil.) -(3)x(7)	Total Bonus Paid [b] ($ mil.)	% Change in Bonus[c] (8)/(9) x100%
Model	Period								
A3'	I	94	-12	na	na	-$ 12	+$ 1	$1027	+0.1%
	II	66	2283	na	na	+2283	-106	2556	-4.1
	III	98	11915	na	na	+11915	-1168	10056	-11.6
	Total	258					-$1272	$13639	-9.3%
A4'	I	94	-.23	12.64	12.87	-$ 80	+$ 8	$1027	+0.8%
	II	66	.12	14.65	14.53	+261	-17	2556	-0.7
	III	98	.59	15.79	15.20	+3217	-251	10056	-2.5.
	Total	258					-$ 260	$13639	-1.9%

Estimates for lost bonus payments in Period IV due to joint bidding ban:

Actual amount of high bids in Period IV ($ mil.)	$5653
Range of % lost due to ban (see text)	1.9% to 11.6%
Range of dollar losses ($ million)	$109 to $742

Table A-16: Estimated Change in Government Revenues from Banning Major Joint Ventures.

[a] Total number of wins by joint ventures with two or more of the seven majors in each period.

[b] Total bonus payments by all bidders in each period.

[c] Estimated change in bonus in the presence of a hypothetical ban on majors with two or more majors, as a percentage of total bonus payments.

which represents 0.5% to 10.2% of the $8.6 million in bonuses col-
lected in those sales.

The sample used in Table A-16 is larger than that of Chapter IV,
and includes 24 sales, and 258 tracts won by joint ventures with
two or more majors. For the three periods together, the $260 million
to $1272 million in estimated losses represents 1.9% to 9.3% of the
$13.6 billion in bonuses collected in all those sales.

The lower part of Table A-16 estimates the effects of the joint
bidding ban in period IV. The high and low percentages of 11.6% and
1.9% come from considering only the figures for period III and periods
I - III averaged. Periods I and II alone were not used because it
was felt that they were less applicable to period IV. The dollar
losses due to banning joint ventures with two or more majors in period
IV range between $109 million and $742 million, compared to the
$5.6 billion actually paid in period IV.

As noted in Chapter IV (pp. 141 ff), this calculation represents
the maximum possible loss, since it does not address the possibility
that the number of bidders per tract, and the level of winning bid
both might rise as a consequence of the ban. Furthermore, to the
extent that the government's objectives include more than maximizing
bonus dollars received, the ban might be less costly than these
figures indicate. For example, if part of the government's object
is to diversify the holdings of OCS tracts, then lower winning bids
might be acceptable. Furthermore, if the government's objectives
include a more rapid development of the hydrocarbon resources of the
OCS, through an increased pace of leasing, then lower bids might

result, which would be in no way a consequence of the joint bidding ban. Appendix B examines several of the issues surrounding the successes and failures of the 1975 ban.

FOOTNOTES

1. Three data files, designated LPR-5, LPR-10 and LRP-19 are
   available from John Lohrenz, Chief, Applied Research and
   Analysis Section, Conservation Division, U.S. Geological
   Survey, MS608, Building 85, Denver Federal Center, Denver,
   Colorado 80225.

2. These time periods correspond to those used in Dougherty and
   Lohrenz, "Statistical Analysis of Solo and Joint Bids for
   Federal Offshore Oil and Gas Leases," Society of Petroleum
   Engineers Journal (April, 1978) 87-95. The adjusted data
   set used in Chapter IV includes 2317 bids in period I, 2337
   bids in period II and 1815 bids in period III, for a total
   of 6469 bids. (See Table 4-1, p. 100.)

3. This is a different division of PBJV's than was employed in
   Chapter IV section 5 (p. 128). The disaggregation used here
   facilitates discussion of the 1975 joint bidding ban, which
   applies to all joint ventures with two or more majors.

4. Tables A-11 and A-13 also serve to illustrate the high prices
   paid in period III by joint ventures with two or more bidders.

APPENDIX B: A NEW LOOK AT THE BAN ON JOINT BIDDING
FOR OFFSHORE OIL[1]

1. Introduction

Since 1954, when the U. S. Government began its auctions of
OCS leases, an increasingly popular form of bidding has been that
of the consortium, or joint venture. In 1975, in response to
growing concerns over potential anticompetitive effects, the
Department of Interior imposed a partial ban on joint venture
bidding by seven major oil companies. This appendix examines
some of the arguments which were presented as justification for
the 1975 ban, and examines whether the ban should be retained in
its present form. In particular, this appendix suggests that the
supposed anticompetitive advantages accruing to the major oil
companies also appear to benefit smaller companies. It also
finds that, ceteris paribus, the overall competitiveness of OCS
lease sales has, in important ways, improved since the joint
bidding ban was imposed in 1975.

Section 2 of this appendix contains a brief description of
the history of joint bidding in OCS sales, and a discussion of
the 1975 ban. Section 3 reviews a study by Gaskins and Vann which
was the the principal study leading to the adoption of the ban,
several subsequent critiques of that Study, and other analyses of
the effects of the ban.[2] Next, Section 4, contains a new look at
the ban, and at the value of the information gained by joint
venture members, both major and non-major companies. Section 5

concludes this appendix with some suggestions regarding the future of the joint bidding ban, and some recommendations for further research.

2. Joint Bidding in OCS Sales

From 1954 through July, 1979, there were 49 federal OCS sales. In those sales, 12,490 bids, totalling over $62 billion were received on a total of 3931 offshore tracts. Of those bids, 3524 high bids totalling nearly $24 billion were accepted by the government.

Table B-1 presents some descriptive statistics of the 49 sales covered in this appendix, grouped into the same four time periods used in Appendix A, the last of which covers the period since the joint bidding ban took effect. The data used in this appendix again come from the LPR tapes maintained by the United States Geological Survey (USGS).[3] While Appendix A restricted attention to only wildcat tracts, this appendix considers all types of tracts, including wildcat, drainage, and development.[4]

Of interest in Table B-1 is the percent of all bids submitted by joint ventures. This percentage reached a peak during the period immediately prior to the joint bidding ban, when nearly two bids in three were submitted by some type of joint venture. As can be seen in column (9) of the table, the ban applied only to joint ventures involving two or more of seven major oil companies. As noted by Dougherty and Lohrenz, the ban seems to have reduced the total number of joint ventures (column (6) in Table B-1), and sent majors in search of other partners.[5] This is indicated by the drop in the percentage of bids by joint

(1)	(2)	(3)[a]	(4)	(5)[b]	(6)	(7)	(8)	(9)
		Number of	Number of	Total Number				Percentage of Total Bids Placed By Joint Ventures[c]
Sale Dates	Number of Sales	Tracts Bid On	Tracts Leased	of Bids Rec'd	All JVs	JVs, No Majors	JVs, 1 Major	JVs, 2+ Majors
1954-66	15	1113	1062	3055	31.2%	15.4%	6.5%	9.3%
1967-71[d]	9	612	540	2733	45.6%	33.2%	5.6%	6.8%
1972-75[d]	11	1154	986	3787	65.1%	37.2%	20.0%	7.9%
1975-79	14	1052	936	2915	57.8%	29.2%	28.6%	0.0%[e]
All	49	3931	3524	12490	50.8%	29.1%	15.6%	6.2%

Table B-1: Joint Venture Activity in OCS Sales

a/ Including tracts on which the government rejected bids.
b/ Including rejected bids.
c/ The seven "majors" are Exxon, Gulf, Mobil, Shell, Standard of California, Standard of Indiana, and Texaco.
d/ Through 7/29/75, after which the joint bidding ban took effect.
e/ Zero, since the ban prohibits such joint ventures.

ventures with no majors involved, and the increase in the number of joint ventures with one major.

Specifically, the ban states that any bid placed by a joint venture containing "two or more persons who are on the effective List of Restricted Joint Bidders..." will be automatically disqualified. The list includes all companies with world wide daily hydrocarbon production in excess of the equivalent of 1.6 million barrels of oil. The list, since its inception, has included eight companies: Exxon, Gulf, Mobil, Shell, Standard of California, Standard of Indiana, Texaco, and British Petroleum, although only the first seven of these have participated in OCS sales.[6]

While Table B-1 indicates that a relatively small percentage of all bids were placed by joint ventures with two or more of the seven majors, it was concern over the effects of such joint ventures on the competition for leases, and on competition in the oil industry in general, that led to the ban. Indeed, joint ventures with two or more majors have tended to win with a much higher percentage of their bids than other types of joint ventures. Table B-2 shows that for all periods, joint ventures with two or more majors won with 38.9% of their bids, compared to 23.4% and 34.3% for joint ventures with no majors or one major, respectively. The question of why consortia including several majors do so well naturally arises.

The concern over the effects of joint ventures, however, went beyond the bidding performance of the ventures themselves. Majors also appeared to do better on their solo bids, winning

Percent of Bids Ranking Number One, Placed By:

Sale Dates	All Bidders (Solo and Joint)	Joint Ventures, with:		
		No Majors	One Major	Two or More Majors
1954-1966	36.4%	27.7%	45.7%	37.7%
1967-1971	22.4	15.8	26.3	38.5
1972-1975	30.4	23.1	33.6	40.3
1975-1979	36.1	29.6	33.6	----
All	35.5%	23.4%	34.3%	38.9%

Table B-2: Relative Success of Various Types of Joint Ventures[a]

a/ See notes for Table B-1.

more frequently, and facing, on average, less competition than
their smaller rivals. Table B-3 illustrates the problem, showing
that over the 25 years of OCS sales, majors bidding alone won
with 39% of their bids, compared to only about 30% for
non-majors. The difference in winning percentages is most
pronounced for the period immediately preceding the bidding ban
(1972-1975), when majors won with nearly 45% of their bids, while
non-majors were successful with only about 28% of their solo
bids. Furthermore, as columns (4) and (5) of the table indicate,
majors faced on average fewer competitors than non-majors.

Tables B-2 and B-3 suggest that majors win more frequently
than non-majors on both their joint and solo bids. Table B-3
also suggests that majors face less competition on average, at
least on their solo bids. These successes by majors have led to
questions concerning the competitive implications of allowing
majors to combine in joint ventures. One explanation of the
majors' successes, apparently accepted by the Department of
Interior in establishing the ban on joint bidding by majors, was
developed by Gaskins and Vann, and has been called the
information hypothesis. Briefly, the information hypothesis
holds that majors, when they combine with one another, obtain
information which gives them an unfair competitive advantage. [7]

3. The Information Hypothesis

Not only were joint ventures with two or more majors
relatively successful with their bids, both joint and solo, but a
study by Gaskins and Vann indicated that their success was not
due to their paying higher prices for the tracts which they won. [8]

	(1)	(2)	(3)[a]	(4)	(5)
		Number	Winning	Average	Average
	Sale	of Solo	Solo	Competition	Competition
	Dates	Bids	Bids (%)	per Bid	per Win
Majors:	1954-66	1275	40.6%	3.2	1.5
	1967-71	667	27.0%	6.8	3.5
	1972-75	535	44.9%	3.2	1.4
	1975-79	597	43.9%	3.2	1.6
	All	3074	39.0%	4.0	1.8
Non-Majors:[b]	1954-66	821	32.3%	4.0	1.9
	1966-71	723	23.9%	6.4	2.3
	1972-75	716	28.2%	4.6	1.5
	1975-79	622	41.0%	3.2	1.4
	All	2882	31.1%	4.6	1.7

Table B-3: Relative Success of, and Average Number of
Competitors Facing, Majors and Non-Majors on Their Solo Bids

a/ Including high bids rejected by the government.
b/ Excluding 185 low "noise" bids. See note (a) to Table B-7.

To the contrary, the Gaskins-Vann study indicated that the majors were actually winning tracts on more favorable terms than other bidders. This apparent contradiction between higher success ratios and lower winning bids, as well as the other elements of the majors' bidding success, was explained by Gaskins and Vann in what has been called the "information hypothesis." This hypothesis held that in the formation of joint ventures, major oil companies obtained information about where rival bidders intended to bid. With this added information, majors were able to win tracts on more favorable terms than bidders without such added information.

Gaskins and Vann's primary results are contained in their Table IV, which is in part reproduced here, as Table 4. They examine the ratio of winning bid to the pre-sale estimate of tract value prepared by the U. S. Geological Survey (USGS). When this ratio is broken down by type of bidder (major vs. non-major), and the total number of bids per tract, Gaskins and Vann note two trends in the data. First, the ratio of winning bid to the USGS pre-sale estimate is positively correlated with the number of bids received on the tract. Second, for tracts receiving the same number of bids, majors tend to win with bids that are a smaller multiple of the USGS pre-sale estimate. After reviewing the evidence, Gaskins and Vann conclude:

> These findings support the hypothesis that the observed tendency of the ratio of the high bid to the USGS estimate to increase with the number of bidders is at least partially accounted for by the flow of information between major bidders.[9]

It was largely on the basis of this study that the Department of

Number of Bidders	All Companies	Majors	Non-Majors
1	1.04	0.66	1.12
2	1.55	1.45	2.14
3 to 4	1.90	2.23	1.57
5 to 7	2.59	1.84	6.89
8 plus	6.09	5.71	10.07

Table B-4: Gaskins and Vann's Table IV --- Ratios of High
Bids to Estimated Values for Selected Groups of Bidders
for March, 1974 Sale[10]

the Interior implemented the ban in 1975.

The Gaskins and Vann analysis has drawn a number of responses, including ones from Mobil Oil Corp.,[11] and from the American Petroleum Institute,[12] Dougherty and Lohrenz,[13] and Millsaps and Ott.[14] These critics agree that one major error with the Gaskins-Vann study was its interpretation of the correlation between the number of bidders on a tract, and the ratio of winning bid to USGS estimate. Indeed, such a correlation is inevitable whether or not the information hypothesis is correct.

What Gaskins and Vann failed to appreciate is that the USGS estimate of tract value is, like any bidder's pre-sale estimate of tract value, just that -- an estimate. The estimate may be low, or it may be high. If the USGS estimates are good (unbiased) they should on average be right. Nevertheless, because they are only estimates, and subject to error on any specific tract, it is not surprising to find the observed correlation between number of bidders and the ratio of winning bid to USGS estimate, for the following reason. Suppose that on a particular tract, the USGS estimate was particularly optimistic (i.e., high). Two related events are likely to occur. First, bids received on that tract, including the winning bid, are likely to look low, compared to the government's estimate. Second, there are likely to be fewer bids on that tract than on a more valuable tract. Thus, because of the random variation in the government's pre-sale estimates, there must be a correlation between the number of bids on a tract, and the ratio of the winning bid to the USGS estimate.

One significant part of the Gaskins and Vann analysis which is not refuted by the above argument is the fact that among tracts with the same number of bidders, majors consistantly won with bids which were a smaller proportion of the USGS estimate than non-majors. Assuming that USGS estimates are in fact unbiased, and if all bidders were in possession of identical information, then one would expect that on average, all types of bidders would have the same ratio of winning bid to USGS estimate. Gaskins and Vann's results suggest that for some reason, perhaps due to superior information on which tracts will be receiving more bids, majors do win tracts on more favorable terms. Section 4 of this appendix will be devoted to looking for more evidence of the information hypothesis.

Millsaps and Ott took a different approach to testing the information hypothesis. They sought to construct and test a model which would explain the variations in the probability that a firm would win with a solo bid, partly in terms of the amount of information that the firm had.[15] Their information measure consisted of the number of times a major oil company bid in a joint venture with one or more other majors. They restricted their attention to solo bids, assuming that bidders who did gain superior information would probably want to keep it to themselves.

In finding that their information variable contributed nothing to the explanation of the probability of winning, Millsaps and Ott claimed that their study, in conjunction with the other critiques of Gaskins and Vann, had once and for all laid the information hypothesis to rest, and had furthermore eliminated "any empirical or theoretical basis for the joint bidding ban."[16]

Their model involves a regression of the probability of winning with a bid on several variables, including the level of information (number of joint bids placed in a sale with other majors), and the number of competing bids on the tract. They found, not surprisingly, that the probability of winning was inversely related to the number of competing bids. They also found that the amount of information had a negative, but not significant effect on the probability of winning.

One difficulty with their model is the possibility of multicollinearity among their independent variables. Recall that one important implication of the information hypothesis is that the number of bids on a tract itself depends on the amount of information that a bidder has, since such information may enable the bidder to avoid tracts with more competition. Thus, as will be shown in the next section, there tends to be a negative correlation between the average number of bidders facing a firm on its solo bids, and the number of joint venture partners that firm had in the rest of the sale. This correlation could account for Millsaps and Ott's failure to find support in their study for the information hypothesis.

4. A New Look At The Information Hypothesis

The information hypothesis asserts that during joint venture negotiations, bidders may learn what tracts their partners are interested in, and therby may be able to avoid some competition if they choose to place some bids outside the partnership. While Gaskins and Vann are credited with formulating this hypothesis, as noted in the preceeding section, they looked only at indirect evidence in trying to judge its validity, as did Dougherty and Lohrenz. Millsaps and Ott used a more direct approach, by developing an index of the potential information gained by a joint venture member. They used that index in a regression analysis to explain the probability that a firm would win on one of its solo bids, hypothesizing that, _ceteris_ _paribus_, bidders with more information should have a higher chance of winning. Their analysis assumed, however, that the number of bidders on a tract was independent of the amount of information a bidder possessed, which contradicts one of the main points of the information hypothesis.

This section tests for the effects of information gathered by joint venture participants, both in the ability of those participants to win on their solo bids, and in the amount of competition which they face on their bids. Furthermore, the information hypothesis of Gaskins and Vann is extended to see if non-majors as well as majors benefit from information gathered in joint venture negotiations. Any firm that, in a single sale, bids in a partnership for some tracts, and bids solo for other tracts, might well benefit from knowing something of its partners' bidding intentions.

After describing the general methods to be employed, this section contains three pieces of analysis. First, the conventional information hypothesis will be re-examined, as it applies to major firms only. Second, the possibility that majors might gather information from both majors and non-majors is considered. Finally, the ability of non-majors as well as majors to take advantage of information gained from bidding partners is investigated. The analysis shows that both majors and non-majors gain information regarding tract value when they negotiate with other bidders, and as a consequence, face less competition on their solo bids.

Following Millsaps and Ott, only solo bids by firms are analyzed. This amounts to assuming that any information gained in joint negotiations would be of most value if kept to one's self. That is, if firm A wanted to bid on a tract, and it learned in negotiations that none of its partners intended to bid on that tract, then if firm A bids on that tract, it will most likely be a solo bid, rather than with some other joint venture.

The index of information to be used differs from that used by Millsaps and Ott, although it was considered by them.[17] Their index was the total number of bids in a sale placed by a major in partnership with one or more other majors. This fails to capture the number of different sources of information open to a bidder. For example, a value of 8 for their index could mean 8 joint bids with one other major, or 2 bids each with 4 other majors. The latter case would seem to provide a greater opportunity for gathering information.

The measure of information used in this study is simply the number of other firms a firm had contact with through a joint venture in a sale. In the example of the previous paragraph, 8 joint bids with the same partner would yield a value of 1, while 2 bids with each of 4 partners would give the firm an information index of 4 for that sale. The particular form of the information index is especially important in the later part of the analysis, when the total number of firms contacted in joint ventures (rather than just major firms contacted) is used.[18]

The procedure used to test the information hypothesis is to look at all solo bids, and to examine what happens to firms' winning percentage, and the average number of competitors faced by firms, as the information index (number of joint venture contacts) increases.

The general proceedure used in the analysis is as follows:

1. For each firm in a sale, the number of joint venture contacts was counted. This placed firms in categories, according to their information index, or opportunities to gain information.

2. The total number of solo bids placed by firms in each information category was counted, along with the number of first place bids, and the number of competing bids received on each tract. Note that first place bids are not necessarily winning bids since the government occasionally rejects bids on a tract as being too low. For the purposes of testing the information hypothesis, it does not matter whether or not bids were rejected, and all bids are included in the analysis.

3. The numbers of solo bids, and numbers of competitors were next aggregated by information category across sales, into four time periods, corresponding to the periods used in Tables B-1 and B-2. Of chief concern is the number of contacts a bidder had in a particular sale. Thus, in the aggregation process, one bidder might fall into different categories for different sales, if it had different numbers of contacts in different sales.

4. Finally, the percentage of bids ranking number one, the average number of competitors on all bids, and the average number of competitors on first place bids were computed for each time period, and each information category.

Data for the analysis in this appendix comes from the LPR-5 and LPR-10 data tapes maintained and distributed by the U. S. Geological Survey, Conservation Division.[19] These tapes contain information on OCS leases, including the identity of each bidder, the bid level, USGS pre-sale estimates, a history of tract development, including wells drilled, and a history of production from each tract.

If the information hypothesis is correct, the analysis should reveal two things. Bidders with more information (more contacts) should first rank number one with a higher percentage of their bids, and second, face less competition than those bidders with less information.

a. Joint Ventures of Majors with Other Majors

Gaskins and Vann argued that information exchanged among majors was of the most concern to policy makers. The first part of the analysis deals, then, with this original version of the information hypothesis. In this part, the information index reflects only contacts that majors had with other majors in a sale. Zero contacts indicates not that a firm never bid in a joint venture, but rather that it never bid in a joint venture with another major. Table B-5 presents the results of analysis of the effects of contacts among majors.

In period I, Table B-5 shows relatively few contacts among majors who also placed solo bids. Of the 1275 solo bids by majors in this period, 1072, or 84% were placed by majors which had no other majors as a partner in the sale in which the bid was

(1)	(2)	(3)	(4)	(5)	(6)	(7)
Period	Sale Dates	Infor- mation Index (Contacts)	Number of (Solo) Bids	High Bids (in %)	Average Compet. per Bid	Average Compet. per High Bid
I	1954-66	0	1072	40.4%	3.2	1.5
		1	170	41.2%	3.5	1.7
		2+	33	42.4%	2.2	1.2
II	1967-71	0	265	21.5%	7.7	3.3
		1	369	29.3%	6.3	3.7
		2+	33	45.4%	4.8	3.1
III	1972-75	0	296	50.0%	3.0	1.4
		1	98	32.6%	4.5	2.2
		2+	141	42.6%	2.8	0.8
IV	1975-79	0	597	43.9%	3.2	1.6
		1	0	---	---	---
		2+	0	---	---	---
All	1954-79	0	2230	40.4%	3.7	1.6
		1	637	33.0%	5.3	2.8
		2+	207	43.0%	3.0	1.3

Table B-5: Relative Success and Average Number of Competitors of Major Oil Companies on their Solo Bids, by Number of Contacts

placed. Nevertheless, there is a slight tendency for the winning percentage (column (5)) to rise with the number of contacts in period I. Period II most clearly exhibits the trend in winning percentage that the information hypothesis would predict. In period III, and for all four periods taken together, the relationship between contacts and winning percentage does not appear to be linear, with the percentage declining as number of contacts rises from 0 to 1, then rising for two or more contacts.

The evidence with regard to the number of competitors faced is also not entirely in conformance with the information hypothesis. In almost every period, for both all bids tendered, and all winning bids, the average number of competing bids is higher for majors which had exactly one major partner than for those with no such partner. Majors with two or more contacts, however, faced substantially less competition on their bids.

b. Joint Ventures of Majors with Majors and Non-Majors

If majors are supposed to be able to derive information from other majors which aids them in knowing where to place their solo bids, it seems possible that they might also obtain similarly useful information from a joint venture contact with a non-major as well. The relative success of majors on their solo bids, grouped by the total number of contacts with all other firms which the bidder had in a sale, is examined in Table B-6.

Table B-6 shows rather mixed results. Only in period II is there a clear improvement in winning percentage as the number of contacts increases, although for the entire period studied firms with one or more contacts in a sale do exhibit the tendency for

(1) Period	(2) Sale Dates	(3) Information Index (Contacts)	(4) Number of (Solo) Bids	(5) High Bids (in %)	(6) Average Compet. per Bid	(7) Average Compet. per High Bid
I	1954-66	0	958	41.5%	3.2	1.5
		1 - 5	317	37.5%	3.3	1.6
		6 -10	0	---	---	---
		11+	0	---	---	---
II	1967-71	0	241	18.7%	8.2	3.9
		1 - 5	426	31.7%	5.9	3.4
		6 -10	0	---	---	---
		11+	0	---	---	---
III	1972-75	0	164	50.0%	3.4	1.3
		1 - 5	107	39.2%	4.1	2.1
		6 -10	127	38.6%	3.5	1.7
		11+	137	48.9%	2.1	0.7
IV	1975-79	0	383	46.2%	3.1	1.5
		1 - 5	133	39.1%	3.6	1.8
		6 -10	53	45.3%	3.3	2.1
		11+	28	32.1%	3.1	1.0
All	1954-79	0	1746	40.2%	3.9	1.6
		1 - 5	983	35.4%	4.6	2.4
		6 -10	180	40.6%	3.4	1.8
		11+	165	46.1%	2.2	0.8

Table B-6: Relative Success and Average Number of Competitors of Major Oil Companies on their Solo Bids, by Number of Contacts With All Other Companies (Majors and Non-Majors)

their winning percentage to rise as number of contacts rises. Comparing Table B-6 to Table B-5, it does not appear that contacts with non-majors add to the ability for majors to win on their solo bids.

As in Table B-5, the statistics on average number of competitors faced again first rise, then fall as the number of contacts rises, falling fairly dramatically for bidders which had 11 or more contacts in a sale. For example, in period III, major bidders with 11 or more contacts faced an average of only 0.7 opponents on tracts on which they bid solo and won.

c. Joint Ventures on Non-Majors with Majors and Non-Majors

This part of the analysis continues the thought raised in (b), considering now whether non-majors might also be able to derive information useful to their solo bidding, by entering joint ventures for some of their bids in a sale. The results are presented in Table B-7.

The relationships predicted by the information hypothesis are quite evident in periods II and III, and are present, but not so strongly, for the entire 25 year period. For each of these categories, the winning percentage rises, and the average number of competitors falls, as the number of contacts rises. Periods I and IV fail to uniformly exhibit the expected trends for winning percentage, although the level of competition does decline somewhat as number of contacts rises.

Of particular interest in Table B-7 is the surprising reversal of the effect of number of contacts on winning

(1)	(2)	(3) Infor-mation Index (Contacts)	(4) Number of (Solo) Bids[a]	(5) High Bids (in %)	(6) Average Compet. per Bid	(7) Average Compet. per High Bid
Period	Sale Dates					
I	1954-66	0	651	32.7%	4.2	2.0
		1 - 5	140	35.0%	3.0	1.6
		6 -10	30	10.0%	3.8	1.7
		11+	0	---	---	---
II	1967-71	0	327	18.4%	7.1	3.2
		1 - 5	384	29.4%	5.7	1.9
		6 -10	12	0.0%	8.0	---
		11+	0	---	---	---
III	1972-75	0	275	15.3%	6.2	2.7
		1 - 5	336	35.4%	3.6	1.4
		6 -10	66	37.9%	3.6	0.8
		11+	39	41.0%	2.7	0.9
IV	1975-79	0	203	42.4%	3.5	1.6
		1 - 5	274	44.5%	2.9	1.1
		6 -10	96	34.4%	3.8	2.1
		11+	49	28.6%	2.6	0.6
All	1954-79	0	1456	27.5%	5.1	2.2
		1 - 5	1134	35.5%	4.1	1.5
		6 -10	204	29.9%	4.0	1.5
		11+	88	34.1%	2.6	0.7

Table B-7: Relative Success and Average Number of Competitors of Non-Major Oil Companies on their Solo Bids, by Number of Contacts With All Other Companies (Major and Non-Major)

a/ Excluding a total of 185 low "noise" bids, defined by ln(Bid)<10, or (Bid)<$22,026.

percentage between period III (pre-ban) and period IV (post-ban).
While the predictions of the information hypothesis are supported
in period III, they are not in period IV. Since the 1975 ban had
nothing to do with joint ventures formed by non-majors, one would
not suspect that the change in the trend of winning percentage of
non-majors was attributable to the ban.

Further insight is gained into this surprising result by
referring to Table B-3, which shows the overall winning
percentage of majors and non-majors on their solo bids, without
regard for the number of contacts. During the first three
periods examined, majors won with a much larger percentage of
their solo bids than did non-majors. For example, in period III,
44.9% of major's solo bids were winners, compared to only 28.2%
of non-majors' solo bids. In period IV, however, non-majors
substantially caught up, winning with 41.0% of their solo bids,
to 43.9% for majors. Furthermore, the reason that non-majors
fared better than they had in the past does not appear to be
because majors faced more competition but rather, non-majors
faced less competition than in period III. This is indicated in
columns (4) and (5) of Table B-3, which show that in period IV
the average number of competitors facing non-major solo bids fell
to a level equal to or below the average for majors.

Table B-8 presents another view of why non-majors have been
able to improve their performance. The table shows the average
number of bidders per tract, derived from Table B-1 columns (3)
and (5).

Table B-8 indicates that there has been a steady decline in

Period	Average Number of Bids Per Tract
I	2.7
II	4.5
III	3.6
IV	2.8
All	3.2

Table B-8: Average Number of Bids Per Tract

the number of bids per tract from period II through period IV. From periods III to IV, non-majors seem to have been greater beneficiaries of the declining number of bids per tract than have majors, since non-majors' winning percentage has improved more than that of majors. If the bidding ban were to be responsible for the increased ability of non-majors to win tracts, it should be because majors were forced to face more competition, not because non-majors face less. Thus the bidding ban cannot be credited with the increased success of non-major solo bidders.

Sullivan and Kobrin use evidence similar to that in Table B-8, showing decreased number of bids per tract in the post-ban period, as evidence that the ban has lessened competition in OCS lease sales. Even after controlling for a decrease in tract quality, which they measure by average winning bid, they still find that the average number of bids per tract, ceteris paribus, has declined.

The declining number of bids per tract shown in Table B-8 does not necessarily mean that competition has decreased. First, as Sullivan and Kobrin acknowledge, average tract quality has decreased since the ban took effect. Using a different measure of tract quality, namely the geometric average of the USGS pre-sale estimate of tract value, Table B-9 indicates the decline from period III to IV. In fact, the percent decline in the geometric average pre-sale estimate is very close to the decline in the geometric average of winning bids.

Second, the degree of competition should not be measured solely by the number of bids per tract, or the average winning

Period	Geometric Average Winning Bid[a]	Geometric Average Pre-Sale Estimate[a]
III	15.26	13.43
IV	14.64	12.91
Percent Change from III to IV	-4.06%	-3.87%

Table B-9: Decline in Tract Quality
from Period III to Period IV.

[a]The geometric average is the arithmetic average
of the natural log of the variable.

bid, since other factors influence those measures. Rather, attention should be paid to whether different sale participants are able to effectively compete. Evidence from Tables B-2 and B-3, and from Appendix A, Table A-13, indicates that in the post-ban period, non-majors' winning percentages are closer to the winning percentages of majors (both solo and joint) than in earlier periods. Table B-3 also indicates that on solo bids, in period IV the average number of competitors faced by majors was the same as the average number faced by non-majors (an average of 3.2 competitors per bid). By contrast, in period III, non-majors faced more competition (4.6 competitors per bid) than did majors (3.2 competitors per bid). Although the overall quality of tracts leased in the post-ban period is lower, the level of competition has in important ways been enhanced.

5. Conclusions

Appendix B has re-examined the information hypothesis of Gaskins and Vann, extending it to include both major and non-major oil companies. The evidence presented strongly supports the hypothesis that all bidders -- both majors and non-majors -- gain valuable information from joint venture contacts. Tables B-5, B-6 and B-7 indicate that bidders with more joint venture contacts consistently face less competition when they place solo bids. Another aspect of the information hypothesis is less clear, however. The data do not conclusively indicate that increased numbers of joint venture contacts in a sale permit any class of bidder -- major or non-major -- to have a higher percentage of winning solo bids, although there is a tendency in that direction, particularly in period II.

The small number of competitors faced by bidders with large numbers of contacts has several possible explanations. One explanation is, of course, the information hypothesis. Bidders with large numbers of joint venture contacts in a sale may choose to place their solo bids where they know none of their partners intend to bid, thus avoiding some potential competition.

A second view of the declining number of competitors faced involves the the kinds of tracts that are involved. The analysis considers solo bids that are placed by firms that may also have bidding partners in a sale. Suppose that bidder X has a large number of partners in a sale, and yet X still decides to place a solo bid on tract A. It must be that either X feels that tract A is particularly valuable, and X does not want to have to share the tract with any partners, or none of X's partners express any interest in tract A, and so X is left to bid alone. Of the two possibilities, the latter seems more plausable, since if tract A were particularly valuable, it would also tend to be particularly expensive, and thus, the kind of tract for which a joint bid is most desirable in order to share the expense and the risk.

If the analysis in the preceeding paragraph is correct, then bidders with more partners in a sale do in fact have added information, and Gaskins and Vann are, in a sense, right. Bidders do gain information on where their partners are not interested in bidding, but more importantly, bidders gain information on the true value of the tract. By knowing that other bidders are not interested in a tract, they may revise their own estimate of what the tract is worth. This means that Gaskins and Vann, and Millsaps and Ott did not carry their analysis far enough. Bidders with joint venture contacts may learn something of their partners' bidding intentions, but the reason that they face less competition on their solo bids, is that they know (or at least correctly assume) that they are bidding for less valuable tracts. Bidding on less valuable tracts, and facing fewer bidders, it would not be at all surprising to see these firms winning with greater frequency than firms with fewer contacts (and less information), as the information hypothesis predicts. It would also not be surprising to find bidders with more contacts to be paying lower prices for the tracts that they do win, as the information hypothesis also predicts.

There remain several areas in need of further investigation. First, a revised statement of the information hypothesis holds that a bidder with partners in a sale, actually gains information about the value of some tracts, in addition to the bidding intentions of his partners. If this restatement is correct, then the value of tracts receiving solo bids should decline with the number of joint venture contacts the bidder has. To study this, several measures of tract value could be used. One frequent proxy for tract value is, in fact, the number of bidders on a tract.[20] Other possible measures include the winning bid, the average bid, the USGS pre-sale estimate, and the discounted present value of ultimate production from the tract. All of these measures are available or can be derived from the LPR data tapes.

A second area needing further study is the tendency shown in
Tables B-5 and B-6 for majors, when bidding solo, to do worse
when they have a few partners in a sale than when they either
have none or many (six or more). This seems to suggest that
majors with only a few partners might actually end up bidding
against those partners when placing solo bids, rather than
avoiding them, as the information hypothesis would suggest. The
extent to which majors (and other bidders) end up bidding against
their partners on some tracts could be evaluated, again using
data from the LPR tapes.

Finally, competition for OCS leases is only one small part
of competition in the U.S. oil industry. It is well beyond the
scope of this study to investigate the effects of not only joint
bidding, but other joint operations among oil companies, to see
what, if any, effect those operations have on competition in the
oil industry as a whole. Nevertheless, a satisfactory price and
quantity of petroleum products is the ultimate concern of any
regulatory policy, and it is with that end in mind that policies,
including the partial ban on joint ventures, should be judged.

To sum up, two conclusions emerge from this reconsideration
of the partial ban on joint bidding, and the information
hypothesis which helped promote that ban. First, the analysis of
Section 4 shows that Gaskins and Vann's information hypothesis
applies to both majors and non-majors. All bidders gain
information that partners do not intend to bid on certain tracts,
and that information enables bidders to better estimate the value

of those tracts. As a result, bidders with more joint venture
contacts face less opposition when they place solo bids.

Second, the 1975 ban has enhanced the degree of competition
in OCS sales. Non-major bidders have been faring better relative
to their performance prior to the ban, and relative to the
performance of majors, in terms of the percentage of their solo
and joint bids which win. The facts that both majors and
non-majors have closer winning percentages, and face more nearly
the same number of competing bids, on average, both suggest that
competition has indeed been strengthened since the ban.

FOOTNOTES

1. An earlier version of this Appendix was presented to the Annual
   Meeting of the Eastern Economics Association, Philadelphia, PA,
   April 9-11, 1981.

2. D. W. Gaskins, Jr. and B. Vann, "Joint Buying and the Seller's
   Return--The Case of OCS Lease Sales," in Hearings before the
   Subcommittee on Monopolies and Commercial Law, of the House
   Committee on the Judiciary, Energy Industry Investigation,
   Part I: Joint Ventures (July 30, 1975), pp. 210-220.

3. For tape availability, see Appendix A, footnote 1.

4. See Tables 2-1, A-1 and A-2 for more information regarding the
   types of tracts leased in each sale.

5. E. L. Dougherty and J. Lohrenz, "Statistical Analysis of Solo
   and Joint Bids for Federal Offshore Oil and Gas Leases," Society
   of Petroleum Engineers Journal (April, 1978), p. 93.

6. For a recent statement of the list see

7. The term "information" hypothesis seems to have been adopted
   by S. W. Millsaps and M. Ott, "Information and Bidding Behavior
   by Major Oil Companies for Outer Continental Shelf Leases: Is
   the Joint Bidding Ban Justified?", processed (no date), p. 218.

8. Gaskins and Vann, op. cit., p. 218.

9. Ibid.

10. Ibid.

11. Mobil Oil Corporation, "An Analysis of the Paper, 'Joint Buying
    and the Seller's Return--The Case of OCS Lease Sales', by
    Darius W. Gaskins, Jr. and Barry Vann," in Hearings before the
    Subcommittee on Monopolies and Commercial Law of the House
    Committee on the Judiciary, Energy Industry Investigation,
    Part I: Joint Ventures (July 30, 1975), pp. 235-238.

12. Two related studies were produced by API: P. Kobrin, C. M. Canes
    and P. Murphy, "Is the Ban on Joint Bidding Warranted?", pro-
    cessed (February, 1977), and B. Sullivan and P. Kobrin, "The
    Joint Bidding Ban: Pro- and Anti-Competitive Theories of Joint
    Bidding in OCS Lease Sales," Research Paper #010, American
    Petroleum Institute (August 11, 1978).

13. Dougherty and Lohrenz, op. cit.

14. Millsaps and Ott, op. cit.

15. Ibid., pp. 9ff.

16. Ibid., p. 12.

17. Ibid., p. 11. footnote 21.

18. The record for the maximum number of firms contacted through joint ventures in a single sale is shared by Pennzoil Offshore Gas Operators Co. (POGO) and Pennzoil Louisiana and Texas Offshore, Inc. (PLATO), who, in the May 29, 1974 sale, each contacted 29 other bidders.

19. See note   , Appendix A.

20. See Chapter IV, Section 2, and Appendix A for further discussion of controlling for tract quality.

For Product Safety Concerns and Information please contact our EU
representative GPSR@taylorandfrancis.com Taylor & Francis Verlag GmbH,
Kaufingerstraße 24, 80331 München, Germany

Printed and bound by CPI Group (UK) Ltd, Croydon, CR0 4YY

08/05/2025

01864412-0007